FOLLOWING JESUS
Defining Discipleship in the 21st Century

by
Kelly Brady

EQUIP Publishing

also by Kelly Brady

POCKET THEOLOGY
A guide to the Bible's teaching for those on the go....

FOLLOWING JESUS
Defining Discipleship in the 21st Century

MY DIRTY SHIRT
A Modern Parable of Salvation

GLEN ELLYN BIBLE CHURCH ELDER NOTEBOOK
A Manuel Strengthening Elder Leadership

FOLLOWING JESUS
Defining Discipleship in the 21st Century

Copyright © 2013 by Kelly Brady

First Edition

Cover photo: Rafal Olkis/image #152148512/Photos.com

Published by EQUIP Publishing
www.equippedtoserve.org

Printed in the United States of America

ISBN 13: 978-0615741499
ISBN 10: 0615741495

to
my children

Andrew, Micah and Rachel

May you know the joy of following
Jesus all the days of your life.

Table of Contents

"Come, follow me," Jesus said,
"and I will make you fishers of men."
Matthew 4:19 (NIV)

Introduction

When Simon Peter and his brother Andrew heard Jesus' call to "Come, follow me," there was no mistaking the invitation. Jesus was inviting them to disrupt every aspect of their lives and enter one of the first century's most intimate of relationships, that of discipleship. In that first-century world disciples were those who detached themselves from their own way of life and reattached themselves to a *rabbi* (teacher), becoming like him in every way. The invitation to study with a rabbi was quite literally an invitation to "follow" after him, as first-century disciples would actually parade around behind their teacher. In following the rabbi they would pay attention to every word he spoke and every move he made, sometimes even trying to mimic his mannerisms, but always trying to imitate his conduct, with the ultimate goal being to reflect his character and concerns.

Discipleship meant doing whatever it would take to become like their rabbi, and they gave themselves to this task wholeheartedly. So complete and total was a disciple's commitment to the rabbi that it became the defining element of their character, and the nature of what it means to be a disciple has not changed in over 2000 years. Accepting the invitation to follow Jesus in the twenty-first century is still to be a first-century commitment.

Jesus is still looking for men and women who will disrupt their lives, attach themselves to him in the most intimate of relationships, and begin reflecting his person and carrying out his purposes. While the experience of discipleship will look dramatically different in the twenty-first century, the nature of discipleship has not changed in over two millennia. *Following Jesus* is aimed at defining discipleship in order to help those following after Jesus in the 21st century better understand his call upon their lives.

Making the most of this book...

We will consider *8 Attributes* of a disciple in this book, characteristics that all followers of Jesus will possess in increasing measure. We will also consider *4 Activities* of a Disciplemaking church, those activities essential for churches wanting to make disciples. While these *8 Attributes* and *4 Activities* are not offered as exhaustive lists, they are offered as essential in the lives of Jesus' followers and in churches wanting to help people follow after Jesus.

The *8 Attributes* of a Disciple

Receive Salvation by Grace	Depend on Jesus' Power Fully
Worship in Life Continually	Connect in Fellowship Deeply
Obey Jesus' Teaching Wholly	Love Others Selflessly
Serve with Jesus Passionately	Pursue the Lost Intentionally

The *4 Activities* of a Disciplemaking Church

Proclaiming the Gospel	Restoring the Broken
Equipping Believers	Sending Out Disciples

In an effort to order our thinking, this definition of discipleship is illustrated in the *Disciplemaking Target,* a pictorial representation of Glen Ellyn Bible Church's philosophy of ministry, which was developed by the church's elders (see adjoining page).

Hitting the bull's-eye of the *Disciplemaking Target* means demonstrating the character, conduct, and concerns of Jesus by evidencing these *8 Attributes* in one's life. Toward this end, chapters 1 and 2 will define the outer rim of the *Disciplemaking Target,* addressing the purpose of life, as well as identifying the most fulfilling life. Chapters 3 through 10 will each address one of the *8 Attributes,* while chapters 11 through 14 will address the *4 Activities* of a Disciplemaking church.

Group discussion questions are provided at the end of each chapter. It is my prayer that the Holy Spirit will use this book to encourage and strengthen you as a follower of Jesus Christ.

GEBC's Disciplemaking Target

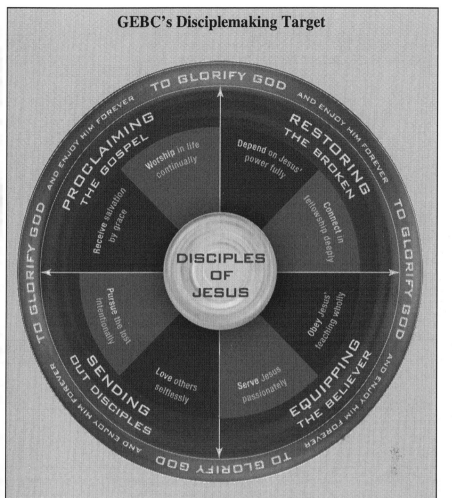

Message
We were created to glorify God and enjoy Him forever.

Mission
We glorify God by making disciples of Jesus Christ.

Method
We make disciples by imitating Jesus Christ's Disciplemaking
activities of: Proclaiming the Gospel, Restoring the Broken,
Equipping the Believer and Sending Out Disciples.

Part I

Hitting the Disciplemaking Target

What are God's purposes for our lives? How do we fulfill God's purposes and experience the most enjoyment in life? Part one of *Following Jesus* tackles these important questions!

Looking at the *Disciplemaking Target*, the words G*lorify God* on the outer perimeter (page xi) remind us that our overall life purpose and discipleship focus should be aimed at glorifying God!

As followers of Jesus Christ, his interests and the interests of his bride, the church, are to be our primary goal and our preeminent passion. Certainly, God's desire is that I become fully me and you become fully you, but God knows that happens only as we are committed to his glory. Jesus said, "Whoever wants to save his life will lose it, but whoever loses his life for me will find it" (Matthew 16:25). In other words, a full life is found only as we live for the glory of Jesus, and death is promised if we do not live for his glory.

The good news of God's purposes for our lives is that what brings him the greatest glory also brings us the greatest joy. For this reason, our stated purpose in the outer circle of the *Disciplemaking Target* is not only to *Glorify God*, but also to *Enjoy Him Forever*. Discipleship means not only living for God's glory, but also experiencing God's enjoyment. King David wrote, "Delight yourself in the Lord and he will give you the desires of your heart" (Psalm 37:4). Only in a life dedicated to Jesus do we find true and lasting enjoyment. This is not to say that living for God's glory will always be fun or easy, but that joy will always be the outcome.

Chapter 1
Here Comes the Groom

The Christian ideal has not been tried and found wanting;
it has been found difficult and left untried.
G.K. Chesterton

Sean and Melissa began dating during their sophomore year of college, and Sean popped the question just before graduation in May. Melissa's dream had always been to have a Christmas wedding, so they set their date for the following December. Gary, Sean's best friend since the ninth grade, was excited for the couple. Although things had not worked out between Gary and his girlfriend, he was eager to serve as Sean's best man and expected Sean and Melissa to live happily ever after. At least that is what Gary told himself, and for the longest time that is what he genuinely felt.

At the engagement party, though, Gary's feelings began to change. He felt jealous of Sean and wished he were engaged. Melissa looked so beautiful that evening and on more than one occasion during the party he found himself dreaming about what it would be like if he were engaged, and not in general, but in specific—that is, to Melissa.

In the months leading up to the wedding Gary's jealousy grew and his actions became more and more selfish. He took every opportunity he had to flirt with Melissa, hoping that she might reciprocate. At first Melissa innocently enjoyed the extra bit of attention, believing Gary's flirting was simply an expression of the love he had for Sean and the excitement he shared for their engagement. As time wore on though, Melissa's feelings for Gary changed as well. She started to look forward to Gary's playfulness and flattery and even began to make excuses to seek him out.

Melissa could tell that their flirting was bothering Sean, but she figured that he would say something to Gary if he wanted it to stop. She was not going to put a stop to it. With graduation looming and all the wedding plans to manage, life had become almost unbearably stressful and Gary's overtures were actually a welcome distraction to juggling the many tedious details. Besides, she was sure that they would never cross the boundary of physical contact.

After an eight-month engagement, the wedding was only two weeks away when Gary showed up at Sean's house to meet for a tuxedo fitting. Sean was stuck in a meeting at work and would not be home until late; instead, Melissa happened to be there dropping off some food. They did not expect to see one another, or to be alone together. Gary had expected to meet Sean.

That evening, alone in the house, Gary and Melissa consummated their relationship with one of the greatest betrayals possible—infidelity shared between the bride and the best man. Few wounds cut as deep as the betrayal of a man's bride with his best friend, but eight months of unchecked flirting between Gary and Melissa ultimately progressed to an evening filled with selfishness and adultery.

Here Comes the Groom

The Bible is divided between Old and New Testaments. The Old Testament is the story of God's old covenant (agreement) with the nation of Israel. The New Testament is the story of God's new covenant offered to all people through the death of Jesus Christ. John the Baptist is significant because his ministry stood at the crossroads of these two covenant eras. After 400 years of silence between the close of the Old Testament and the open of the New Testament, John the Baptist announced the coming of God's Messiah—Jesus Christ.

Everywhere John the Baptist went large crowds gathered, with many responding to his message by confessing their sins and being baptized. It was an unprecedented revival. Nothing like it had happened in four centuries—that is until Jesus began to preach.

When Jesus began to preach, John the Baptist's crowds began to shrink. Not only were the crowds drawn to Jesus, but some of John the Baptist's own disciples defected in order to follow after Jesus. The fisherman Andrew was one of John the Baptist's disciples who left to follow Jesus, bringing his brother Simon Peter with him (John 1:35-42). Tradition also holds that the disciple John, the one who later wrote the Gospel of John, was also originally a disciple of John the Baptist.

Between the shrinking crowds and defecting disciples, those who remained with John the Baptist were filled with jealousy. The influence they had worked so hard to gain was slipping away, and they did not want to share the spotlight with Jesus. After all, since John the Baptist had baptized Jesus, should not Jesus be funneling followers to John, rather than stealing his audiences and disciples? Fed up with their dwindling influence, John the Baptist's remaining disciples came to him and said, "Rabbi, that man who was with you on the other side of the Jordan—the one you testified about—well, he is baptizing, and everyone is going to him" (John 3:26). John the Baptist's reply?

> The bride belongs to the bridegroom. The friend who attends the bridegroom waits and listens for him, and is full of joy when he hears the bridegroom's voice. That joy is mine, and it is now complete. He must become greater; I must become less. John 3:29-30 (NIV)

The bride belongs to the bridegroom. Sometimes the most obvious truths are the most difficult to embrace. When encouraged by his disciples to compete with Jesus for the attention of the crowds and the fidelity of his disciples, John the Baptist reminds them that the best man's role is to wait upon and listen for the arrival of the groom, not vie with him for the bride's affection. The best man should be full of joy for the groom, not full of envy and self-interest. The groom's interests and honor should be the best man's highest priority.

Competing with Jesus

Jesus described those who will enter heaven as attendants at a wedding who are wisely prepared for the groom's arrival, while he compared those who will not enter heaven to wedding attendants foolishly unprepared for the groom's arrival (Matthew 25:1-13). Jesus is the groom and his bride is the church. We are to serve as Jesus' attendants, caring for the bride as we anticipate the coming wedding day (Revelation 19:7).

Gary and Melissa's betrayal illustrates the point made by John the Baptist. Living as a disciple of Jesus Christ means living for the glory of the bridegroom, not for our own glory. Discipleship means accepting the unique responsibility of awaiting the groom's arrival and tending to the needs of his bride as the groom delays. Too many are eager to be a part of the church, the bride, looking forward to the wedding reception scheduled for the end of time (Matthew 22:1-14), but refuse altogether the invitation to serve as his attendants.

We can tell if our desires are competing with Jesus' glory by checking our calendar, credit card statements, and bank accounts. Identifying to whom or to what we are giving the majority of our time and money quickly establishes whether we are supporting the groom's interests or our own. John the Baptist spoke of being "full of joy" upon hearing the bridegroom's voice. One of the best indicators of whether we are filled with joy *for* Jesus or jealousy *of* Jesus is whether we are eager for his glory in all things. John the Baptist was so eager for Jesus' glory that he could confidently proclaim, "He must become greater, I must become less!" Do we find ourselves competing with Jesus and his glory? Or are we becoming less, so that he can receive increasing glory through our lives? Paul wrote:

> For by him all things were created: things in heaven and on earth, visible and invisible, whether thrones or powers or rulers or authorities; all things were created by him and for him. Colossians 1:16 (NIV)

17

Defining the Target

Looking at the *Disciplemaking Target* used to illustrate a life committed to following after Jesus (page xi), the words g*lorify God* are on the outer perimeter, reminding us that this should be the the overall focus of our lives. Discipleship is a life aimed at bringing God glory! As followers of Jesus Christ, his interests and the interests of his bride, the church, are to be our primary focus and our preeminent passion. Anytime we refuse our role as attendants to the groom we are unfaithful and committing spiritual adultery, garnering attention and affection due only to him. Lest adultery sound too harsh, bear in mind that these were God's words to the prophet Hosea. God said to Hosea, "[Israel] is guilty of the vilest adultery in departing from the Lord" (Hosea 1:2).

The nation of Israel had acted unfaithfully by worshiping idols, and at God's direction Hosea married a prostitute named Gomer, which was to serve as a living example of God's love for his people despite their unfaithfulness. Hosea and Gomer established a home together and had just started a family when she went back to prostitution. If we can imagine our spouse selling their body to others, then we will begin to understand God's feelings of betrayal when we refuse to honor him with our lives (Hosea 1:2).

Unfortunately, John the Baptist's disciples were more eager to follow John the Baptist than to follow Jesus. They struggled to accept their role as attendants to Jesus, because they had no interest in becoming less. Many people still refuse a life of becoming less, and it is often because we misunderstand what "becoming less" entails.

Fully Me

Far too many equate "becoming less" with accepting the status of worthlessness. Too many believe that living for God's glory requires what might be called *worm* theology, named after the lyrics of the childhood song: *Nobody loves me, everybody hates me, so I'm going to eat some worms.* Worm theology is often tied to the doctrine of sin.

If you grew up hearing worm theology preached then you know how damaging it can be. While our sin is loathed *by* God, our sinfulness does not make us any less valuable *to* God! The Bible is clear that although we are steeped in sin, God loves us so much that he gave his only son for us (John 3:16). Paul writes that while we were full of sin Christ died for us (Romans 5:8).

Some respond to worm theology with self-loathing, believing that God would have them hate themselves. However, Luke describes God as a shepherd who leaves the flock to pursue the one lost sheep who strayed (Luke 15:1-7). God comes after us and if we will only come home to him, God stands waiting for us and is eager to run to meet us, throw his arms around us, and celebrate our return (Luke 15:11-32). We are of infinite value to him. No matter how self-destructive or self-sabotaging we may behave, he never values us any less.

Becoming less is also not about becoming less significant! Maybe John the Baptist's disciples refused to follow after Jesus because they felt they would become less significant. But becoming less has nothing to do with denying one's gifts or strengths or calling. We are expected to be good stewards of all that God has entrusted to us (Matthew 25:14-30). The truth is that a life of bringing God glory will involve bearing greater responsibility and making a greater impact.

Finally, becoming less has nothing to do with becoming less of *us*. Becoming less will involve becoming fully ourselves, fully the men and women God created us to be. Too many resist a lifestyle of becoming less because they believe it means the end of themselves. Soren Kierkegaard, the nineteenth-century Danish philosopher wrote, "Now with the help of God, I'll become fully me." Although we are to deny ourselves and take up our cross daily, that is ultimately so we can live in Christ (Matthew 16:25). We deny our sin nature, the selfish and self-seeking desires that are contrary to Christ's glory, but we are to fully become the men and women God intended for us to be. This means that extroverts are to continue to enjoy the party, while introverts are to continue to enjoy the quiet of an evening at home. This means that it is okay for task-oriented people to continue to make lists, while the more people-oriented continue to talk on the phone while instant messaging. In other words, God does not want to change our personality. He wants to change our character. That is what it means to be a disciple and to be increasingly transformed into the image of Jesus, reflecting his character, conduct, and concerns in every area of our lives for the purpose of bringing him glory.

Conclusion

God's desire is that I become fully me and you become fully you, but that only happens as we are committed to glorifying God. Jesus said, "Whoever wants to save his life will lose it, but whoever loses his life for me will find it" (Matthew 16:25). All of the assurances and benefits offered in the Gospels presuppose a life fixed upon bringing glory to Jesus, and none of the assurances or benefits make any sense apart from that commitment.

Group Discussion Questions

1. Considering G.K. Chesterton's quote at the beginning of the chapter, how would you describe the Christian ideal and why might it be difficult?

2. How might Gary and Melissa's story serve as a parable of the relationship Christians have with the church? (Hosea 1:2, Ephesians 5:22-33, Colossians 1:16)

3. Considering the description of John the Baptist's ministry in the Gospels, what evidence is there that he became less? (Matthew 11:1-15; Matthew 14:1-12)

4. Why do you think some of John's disciples refused to become less, and how can you sympathize with their posture?

5. Describe a time in your life when you put aside your own desires, or became less, so that Christ could become greater, as well as a time when you resisted becoming less.

6. How are you currently tempted to compete with Jesus for the position of preeminent importance in life?

7. John spoke of being "full of joy" upon hearing the bride groom's voice. How has serving as an attendant of the groom brought joy into your life? (John 3:29)

8. In the section titled "Fully Me," what were the three misconceptions of becoming less and which, if any, have you labored under?

9. How can others pray for you in the effort of becoming less?

21

Chapter 2
Eeyore Christianity

----

*We are half-hearted creatures, fooling around with drink
and sex and ambition when infinite joy is offered us,
like an ignorant child who wants to go on making mud pies
in a slum because he cannot imagine what is meant by the
offer of a holiday at the sea. We are far too easily pleased.*
C.S. Lewis, The Weight of Glory

Eeyore lives in the Hundred Acre Wood along with Piglet, Roo, Kanga, and Tigger and Pooh. He is the little grey donkey from the *Many Adventures of Winnie-the-Pooh*, stuffed with sawdust and a very "gloomy Gus." He keeps to himself most of the time, living as Eeyore describes it in the Gloomy Place. He is always depressed because he has some problems that plague him. For example, his tail keeps coming off. It's held on only with a tack, and it's always falling off and getting lost. And his house keeps falling down, and he has to rebuild it time and time again. Eeyore lives a joyless existence, and a cloud of discouragement follows him wherever he goes.

Of course, we have all felt depressed like Eeyore at one time or another, but depressed is Eeyore's soul state. The moment joy might appear a cloud of discouragement, which hovers over his head constantly, begins to pour rain. He is a pessimist and grumpy all the time. Ever meet an Eeyore Christian? Worse still, ever meet a follower of Jesus who thought that being dour was somehow more holy than being joyous? Unfortunately, churches are full of people who believe that the dress code for discipleship includes wearing a furrowed brow of concern. Becky Pippert, author of *Out of the Saltshaker*, writes of a sad experience she had before deciding to follow Jesus, an experience of meeting an Eeyore Christian.

I remember once encountering a zealous Christian. His brow was furrowed, he seemed anxious and impatient, and he sounded angry. Then he told me God loved me. I couldn't help noticing the difference between his message and his style. His message was arresting (me, a sinner?) but ultimately appealing (there is a God who loves me deeply). But his style put me off. I recall thinking, If God is so good and loving, then why is this guy so uptight?*

Too often followers of Jesus come off as the proverbial "wet blanket" of life, portraying God as the cosmic killjoy and leaving people wondering what positive impact the gospel has upon our lives. If we believe the good news of the gospel, then our lives will not be ruled by the bad news of this world. The good news of the gospel means that we do not have to live like Eeyore.

The New Testament makes it clear that the gospel is not something simply to be accepted now and enjoyed later, when we get to heaven. The gospel is to be entered into now and experienced fully later when we are in Jesus' presence. Jesus came not just to prepare us for death, but to provide us with life...here, now, today. Jesus said, "I have come that they may have life, and have it to the full" (John 10:10). Life to the full includes joy even in the most dire of circumstances.

The Year of the Lord's Favor

When I first met Erick he wasn't attending our church, but someone asked me if I would help him work through some issues. "Sure," I said, not knowing at all what I was getting myself into. It wasn't until after I had agreed to meet with him that my friend warned me. "Erick," he said, "is a little rough around the edges." "No problem," I said, "I'm happy to meet with anyone." I spoke with Erick later that week and we scheduled our first appointment. I could tell from talking on the phone with him that he had some weighty struggles and that I was in for a challenge.

He arrived early for our appointment and I invited him in right away, figuring we would need all the time we could get together. From the moment he sat down in my office a stream of cusswords poured out of his mouth, profanity the likes of which I had not heard since my days of playing high school sports and hanging out in the boys' locker room. He was not whispering them either. He was shouting profanities near the top of his lungs. Erick continued cussing for about ten minutes, vile words meant to punctuate his anger at his family, as well as his contempt for life and for God.

When he was finally out of breath, the only thing that I could think to say was "I can see that you are angry." The words hung in the air for a moment, as I think he was expecting me to be put off by his swearing and kick him out of my office. Erick had endured decades of emotional and sexual abuse at the hands of various family members. His story was so overwhelming that I next asked him, "What's your hope for getting past all the abuse you have endured?" "I don't know," he said. "I guess my only hope is that God will do something." Then he asked, "Do you think God will help me?" "Absolutely," I answered, and we spent some time praying together, asking God to do just that.

Erick was baptized four years later. Through the help of several friends, trained counselors, and much prayer, God has transformed Erick's outlook on life. He's no longer the very gloomy Gus, who had only swearwords to offer as a commentary on life. While he would tell you that he still has a long way to go, it is obvious to everyone he is filled with real joy. Jesus came that we might have life to the full, which is neither a promise of financial prosperity nor of physical health, but rather the promise of God's presence in our lives. Jesus said:

> The Spirit of the Lord is on me, because he has anointed me to preach good news to the poor. He has sent me to proclaim freedom for the prisoners and recovery of sight for the blind, to release the oppressed, to proclaim the year of the Lord's favor. Luke 4:17-19 (NIV)

We live in the "year of the Lord's favor," in the era of good news of God's salvation! In fact, Paul warned Timothy to be on guard against any who would deny that the power of God is available today. "Have nothing to do with" those types of people, Paul writes! (2 Timothy 3:2-5) In other words, have nothing to do with Eeyore Christians— those who claim to have received the good news of God's salvation but choose to live discouraged, disappointed, and dejected lives.

Defining the Target

In the outer circle of the *Disciplemaking Target*, our stated life purpose is to *Glorify God and Enjoy Him Forever* (page xi). Discipleship means living out the truth that Jesus came that we might have life to the full, and entering his joy despite difficult circumstances.

King David wrote, "Delight yourself in the Lord and he will give you the desires of your heart" (Psalm 37:4). Too often we delight primarily in our achievements or our possessions or in other people, rather than in Jesus, believing that our accomplishments or our acquisitions or our relationships will somehow bring us lasting joy. While our relationship with Jesus includes receiving our positions of authority and our possessions and our friendships as gifts from God, we are to delight ourselves first and foremost in Jesus. We find life to the full only in a relationship with Jesus, and we find it regardless of how meager or ample our achievements, acquisitions, or friendships may be.

Paul reminds us, "In him we live and move and have our being" (Acts 17:28). Only in Jesus do we find real life and a joy that can surmount any amount of disappointment or discouragement. Or course, joy is not something we simply manufacture, but with Jesus in our lives a heart of rejoicing is always available. Paul commands us to "Rejoice in the Lord always" (Philippians 4:4), regardless of our circumstances. Bear in mind that he wrote these instructions from a jail cell. How easy would it have been for Paul to adopt Eeyore's attitude, to look at his circumstances and live in gloom? Yet the book of Philippians is full of joy, despite difficult circumstances. In the book of James we read:

Consider it pure joy, whenever you face trials of many kinds, because you know that the testing of your faith develops perseverance. Perseverance must finish its work so that you may be mature and complete, not lacking anything. James 1:2-4 (NIV)

I realize many of us may not feel like rejoicing. Perhaps you are under a tremendous amount of pressure, or maybe you have suffered a grave loss. It is in these times though that we are called to remain faithful. Do you remember the famous praise received by servants who used their talents wisely? "Well done, thy good and faithful servant," said the master. "You were faithful with a few things, I will put you in charge of many things, now enter into the joy of your master" (Matthew 25:23). Experiencing God's joy is directly linked to our faithfulness, just as it was for the servants who had been entrusted with talents from their master. We find "life to the full" (John 10:10), only as we remain faithful, even in the most dire of circumstances. Another word for faithfulness is obedience. This means that if we are short on joy in our lives, then we should consider a heavy dose of increased obedience. We choose a joy-filled life when we choose obedience.

Real Progress in Faith

Jesus wasn't known to be a "gloomy Gus." Jesus was criticized by religious types for having too much fun, for being the friend of those enjoying the party, the sinners in town. He was seen eating and drinking and carrying on with the irreligious. This drew the fire of the holier-than-thou types who believed their seriousness to be a mark of righteousness. But stern-faced seriousness is not a mark of righteousness. A mark of true righteousness is joy in life and enjoyment of all that God has made, even in the midst of tough circumstances. The prophet Isaiah says that God gives us a "garment of praise instead of a spirit of despair" (Isaiah 61:3). Picture taking off the clothes of fear and anxiety and putting on praise. A mark of real progress in faith is the presence of God's praise on our lips despite the difficulties in life.

Shane Claiborne, author of *The Irresistible Revolution*, writes of growing up in a church that struggled to celebrate God's goodness and of the negative impact it had upon his spiritual growth.

> All the youth used to sit in the back row of the balcony, and we'd skip out on Sunday morning to walk down to the convenient mart for snacks before slipping back into the balcony. I recall thinking that if God was as boring as Sunday morning [worship], I wasn't sure I wanted anything to do with him. And I remember joking with friends that if someone had a heart attack on Sunday morning, the paramedics would have to take the pulse of half the congregation before they would find the dead person. Yes, inappropriate, but funny, and I'm not sure it was far from the truth.*

Christians are often afraid to really celebrate, to let our hair down, and to express our excitement for Jesus. Is there a place for quiet, reverent, and contemplative worship? Absolutely. But we have reason to celebrate every morning, no matter what our circumstances. According to C.S. Lewis, "Joy is the serious business of heaven." God is the most joyous being in the universe and he wants to share his joy with us.

The Eternal Appetite of Infancy

The ability to express joy could be one of the reasons Jesus taught that the kingdom of heaven belongs to those who are childlike. The disciples told the crowds that Jesus did not have time for children, but Jesus corrected them and declared, "Let the children come to me. Don't stop them! For the kingdom of heaven belongs to such as these" (Matthew 19:14). In other words, it's not just that there are children *in* heaven, but that heaven is *owned* by the childlike. In fact, Jesus said, "unless you change and become like little children, you will never enter the kingdom of heaven" (Matthew 18:3). But what does it mean that heaven is filled with the childlike?

After a day of very religious and sober-minded ministry, a day filled with prayer and counseling and study, I found a picture on the kitchen table as I arrived home. It reminded me of the importance of childlike faith. The picture was colored by my daughter Micah, who was six at the time. It was a seascape, and there were starfish on the bottom of the ocean and fish in the water and even fish jumping out of the water. But beyond the obvious elements that belong in a seascape, there was a subtle yet poignant example of why we must all become like little children in order to enter the kingdom of heaven. Each of the fish in the picture had smiles on their faces, silly little grins. Did you know that fish grin? I didn't know that fish grin, but with her keen artistic eye Micah had picked up on some of the more subtle details of aquatic life. Only a child would put smiles on fish!

One of the reasons that heaven belongs to the childlike is that children are typically ready to smile, to celebrate, to play. Children seem to have an innate longing to enjoy life, which is a reflection of God's eternal state of joy. To enter God's kingdom we must be willing to enter his joy. We must set aside our grown-up tendency to live soberly and accept God's invitation to let him carry our burdens. We must set aside our grown-up need to be important and in charge and let him be important, let him do the figuring out, while we go out and play. We must give up control and learn to celebrate. G.K. Chesterton, an English journalist and theologian of the early twentieth century, wrote of the childlike character of God and the barrier that grown-ups have because of it in receiving him.

> ...the sun rises regularly because [God] never gets tired of it rising. And this routine might be due, not to lifelessness, but to a rush of life. This thing I mean can be seen for instance in children, when they find some game or joke that they especially enjoy. A child kicks his legs rhythmically through excess, not absence, of life. Because children have abounding vitality,

because they are in spirit fierce and free, therefore they want things repeated and unchanged. They always say, "Do it again"; and the grown-up person does it again until he is nearly dead or driven half out of his mind. For grown-up people are not strong enough to exult in monotony. It is possible that God says every morning, "Do it again" to the sun; and every evening, "Do it again" to the moon. It may not be automatic necessity that makes all daises alike; it may be that God makes every daisy separately, but has never gotten tired of making them the same. It may be that God has the eternal appetite of infancy; for we have sinned and grown old, and our father is younger than we.

Conclusion

Are you cultivating the eternal appetite of infancy, the child-like strength to exult in monotony? There are few things more child-like than the longing to play and there is possibly no greater demonstration of faith than the enjoyment of God. Enjoyment of life, despite life's difficulties, communicates our trust in God. If we are to enter into the kingdom of heaven then we must become like little children, willing to trust him, enter his rest, and begin enjoying his Son.

Group Discussion Questions

1. How is Becky Pippert's experience of meeting what she described as a "zealous Christian" similar to or different from your experience with Christ's followers?

2. If your habit of rejoicing in all circumstances (Philippians 4:4) were plotted on a continuum, would you fall closer to Eeyore or Paul?

3. Who in your life encourages you to trust God and enjoy him, despite life's difficulties?

4. What types of circumstances most typically undermine your effort to rejoice in the Lord always?

5. How would Jesus' description of himself as the "narrow gate" (Matthew 7:13-14) relate to Paul's assertion that "in him we live and move and have our being" (Acts 17:28)?

6. Jesus identifies four types of people in his *Parable of the Sower*, only one of which ever grows to the point of bearing any type of spiritual fruit. What role does worry and the deceitfulness of wealth play in our fruitlessness? (Matthew 13:1-23)

7. When have you experienced the joy of the Lord as your strength? (Nehemiah 8:9-10)

8. How do you believe we access Jesus' "life to the full"? (John 10:10)

9. How can others pray for you as you process and apply what you have learned in this chapter?

Part 2

The 8 Attributes
of a Disciple

Knowing that God's purposes for our lives are to bring him glory and enjoy him forever, what type of person brings the greatest glory to God and experiences the greatest enjoyment in him? Part two of *Following Jesus* tackles these important questions.

The bull's eye in the middle of the *Disciplemaking Target* (page xi), illustrates that disciples of Jesus are the people who bring the greatest glory to God and who experience the greatest enjoyment in God. Disciples are those committed to a life of following after Jesus, men and women who increasingly emulate the character, conduct, and concerns of Jesus in every area of their lives.

Surrounding the bull's-eye are the *8 Attributes* of a disciple. These are attributes that followers of Jesus will possess in increasing measure as they grow in faithfulness. These *8 Attributes* are not offered as an exhaustive list. However, these 8 are each identified in the Gospels by our Savior as essential marks of discipleship, and chapters 3 through 10 focus on addressing each one of them.

The *8 Attributes* of a Disciple

Receive Salvation by Grace	Depend on Jesus' Power Fully
Worship in Life Continually	Connect in Fellowship Deeply
Obey Jesus' Teaching Wholly	Love Others Selflessly
Serve with Jesus Passionately	Pursue the Lost Intentionally

Chapter 3
Masterpiece in the Making

The world can do almost anything as well as
or better than the church. You need not be a Christian
to build houses, feed the hungry, or heal the sick.
There is only one thing the world cannot do.
It cannot offer God's grace.
Gordon MacDonald*

George Wilson refused a pardon. In 1829 George Wilson and James Porter were convicted of robbing the United States Postal Service and sentenced to death by hanging. Just three weeks before the sentence was carried out, however, Wilson was pardoned by President Andrew Jackson. But in a strange turn of events he refused the pardon, throwing the legal system into a tailspin and forcing the case before the Supreme Court. After much deliberation, the high court ruled that a pardon is without legal effect unless accepted, and the courts have no power to force the pardon upon the convicted.*

Most would agree that Wilson was a fool for refusing the pardon. Yet many reject the pardon offered by God through Jesus Christ. Just as the United States courts held George Wilson accountable for his crimes, God holds all humanity accountable for its sinfulness. Sin is any activity contrary to God's character, and the Bible is clear that all have sinned and stand condemned before God (Romans 3:23). Although we are all under a sentence of death, God is merciful, and he has provided a pardon to any who will accept Jesus' death on the cross as payment for their sin (John 3:16).

The good news of the Gospel is that all we need to do is accept God's pardon. The bad news of the Gospel is that unless we accept God's pardon, we remain condemned (John 3:18).

The apostle Paul described the reality of our situation, writing that we are "dead in our transgressions and sins" (Ephesians 2:1). This means that we and our children, along with our coworkers, neighbors, and friends, are *not* okay simply because we are nice people and engaged in sincere religious activities. Nicodemus was a good person, but to Nicodemus Jesus said, "No one can see the kingdom of God unless he is born again" (John 3:3). Simply put, humanity is not merely sick and in need of a remedy. We are dead because of our sinfulness and in need of life. We must be born again.

Born Again

Jill had attended our church for several years when she shared with me, "I don't like the 'born again' label." She went on to explain that she could not figure out why our church was so insistent on using it. Below is an excerpt from an e-mail she sent me after our meeting. It explains her feelings well.

The words "born again" have always had such a negative con notation for me. It was usually referred to in the same discussion as "Bible banger." Mom would often refer to "those born-agains" as we would pass the big church on the corner where the people would actually go to church for longer than an hour. But it wasn't until you showed me the passage in the Bible, where Jesus tells Nicodemus that he must be born again, that I really did some soul searching and realized that "born again" actually applied to me. It scared me for a while to identify with that statement but I really am a different person now. I don't remember a "moment" that it occurred as every one seemed to feel that most "born agains" do, but I know that I have been "born again". I can feel and often hear the Holy Spirit in my life.

Some resist the born-again label because, like Jill, they misunderstand what Christians are claiming. New birth is not a claim to perfection. It is a claim to imperfection and the need for God's forgiveness and work of repair. God's ultimate goal is that we would be holy, just as he is holy, and receiving God's grace is the first step in this process...and the second and the third and the fourth, etc., etc (1 Peter 1:16).

Jumping Contest

Unfortunately, the message that we must be born again is often resisted, or altogether refused. Many would rather try to manage their sin than to admit their need for God's forgiveness. And admittedly, not all sin is equal. Some sins are worse than others. Murdering someone is obviously worse than gossiping about them, and many reason that they need only to remediate their "lesser" sins in order to be acceptable to God. The truth is that while not all sin is equal, all sin is equally effective in separating us from God. No matter how minor the sin may seem when compared to others, it still separates us from God, which brings death into our lives.

It is natural to compare our sin with the sin others, but comparing our sinfulness is like comparing who can jump closer to the moon. Any National Basketball Association (NBA) player can jump closer to the moon than me, but the comparison of our distances jumped would not adequately portray how far we *both* fall short.

The truth is that while an NBA player may jump three feet higher than I can, neither of us has any hope of landing on the moon. Similarly, no one, no matter how good they may be, has any hope of getting even close to the holiness of God. We will never come anywhere near to God's holy standard of behavior. You might be more righteous than me, but that is not an accurate reflection of how far we fall short of God's holy character. We may be pretty good husbands, fathers, mothers, employees, citizens and neighbors—but you and I are not the standard of perfection.

For this reason, comparing our sinfulness with the sinfulness of others is spiritually dangerous, because it can give a false sense of hope. While I may work on my jumping ability and gain some height in comparison to an NBA player, my best efforts will continue to fall far short. The sin problem in our lives is not something that we are able to fix with more education, or counseling, or socialization, or technology. The belief that we will somehow beat the sin problem on our own through greater effort is simply not true.

Just watch the nightly news. Crime continues to escalate. Most of the nations of the world are engaged at some level in war, and over a billion of the world's population is starving. Humanity is not getting better with time and education. Nothing will alleviate the sin problem in our lives and in our communities except the intervention of God. We must be born again.

Receiving God's Grace

In 1991 Jeffrey Dahmer confessed to sexually abusing, killing, and cannibalizing 17 young men, as well as storing their body parts in his refrigerator and collecting their skulls as trophies. After a short trial, Dahmer was sentenced to 15 consecutive life sentences. No one expected to hear anything about him ever again. But in 1994 his name resurfaced in the news. He had been murdered in the prison gymnasium, beaten to death by one of his fellow inmates. Expecting the talking heads on the news channels to debate whether justice was served or undermined by Dahmer's murder, it was surprising to hear a discussion of his eternal destiny become the focus of mainstream news.

Could a person who had committed such terrible crimes receive God's forgiveness? The debate was spawned by the news that Dahmer had prayed to receive the forgiveness of his sins and was baptized in the prison whirlpool by a Church of Christ minister named Roy Ratcliff. Ratcliff made headlines by commenting that Dahmer was one of his most faithful worshipers. The debate raged. Could God's grace really cover Dahmer's sin? Are not some sins beyond God's forgiveness?

When it comes to experiencing God's grace most gravitate toward one of two extremes. Either we believe that we are in need of very little of it, and we comfort ourselves with memories of good deeds done. Or we believe that we are beyond grace's reach, and we wallow in self-pity and continue in cycles of self-destructive behavior. Dahmer could easily have concluded that he was beyond God's forgiveness. How easy it would have been for Dahmer to believe that Christ's sacrifice was insufficient to cover his sin.

If we believe that we are *above* God's grace, that our righteousness is sufficient to merit salvation, then we effectively diminish God's holiness, not to mention overestimate our righteousness. On the other hand, if we believe that we are *beyond* God's grace, that the death of Christ is insufficient to purchase our forgiveness, then we diminish the significance of Jesus' death on our behalf, acting as if our sins require a greater sacrifice than God provided. In both cases, pride prevents us from experiencing God's gift of grace. Avoiding these extremes is essential to discipleship.

Hitting the Target

Salvation is unmerited, and a life of discipleship begins, ends, and continues solely by receiving God's grace. Paul wrote:

> For it is by grace you have been saved, through faith—and this not from yourselves, it is the gift of God—not by works, so that no one can boast. For we are God's workmanship, created in Christ Jesus to do good works, which God prepared in advance for us to do. Ephesians 2:8-10 (NIV)

Adding to the *Disciplemaking Target* we are using to illustrate a life committed to following after Jesus, *Receive Salvation by Grace* is the first of the *8 Attributes*. Disciples are those who continue by God's grace, as followers of Jesus. We begin and end the journey of faith, based upon the grace of God and nothing else.

Paul wrote that "we are God's workmanship," and the Greek

word for "workmanship" is the word *poiema*, from which we get the word "poem." The idea is that God is at work in us creating something beautiful. We are his work of art, his masterpiece, and it is his grace that shapes. Look at how Paul describes the work of grace in our lives.

> For the grace of God that brings salvation has appeared to all men. It teaches us to say "No" to ungodliness and worldly passions, and to live self-controlled, upright and godly lives in this present age. Titus 2:11 (NIV)

So many Christians accept the grace offered for the forgiveness of their sin, but act as though they are on their own to fix themselves. But there is no bait and switch in Christianity. It's not grace to start and human effort to finish. A life of discipleship is a dependence upon the grace of God from start to finish. It's God's grace—not human effort—that "teaches us to say 'No' to ungodliness."

The good news of the gospel is that we can do nothing to make God love us more or to make him love us less. Let's revel in the acceptance we have experienced through Christ and continue in grace. If you have never confessed your sins to God and asked for God's forgiveness offered through Jesus Christ, then you can pray the prayer in the box to receive God's grace and begin the journey of following Jesus.

Prayer of Forgiveness for Sin

Dear Heavenly Father,

Thank you for your grace shown toward me through Jesus' death on the cross. I confess that I am sinful and I need your forgiveness, and I accept by faith Jesus sacrifice on my behalf.

Thank you for new birth and help me now to follow after Jesus and continue in your grace.

Amen.

Jars of Clay

If you have prayed to receive God's forgiveness through Jesus Christ, the apostle Paul describes it as receiving a treasure. He wrote to the believers in the city of Corinth, "We have this treasure in jars of clay to show that this all-surpassing power is from God and not from us" (2 Corinthians 4:7). Paul does not say that we are jars of gold, or silver or even bronze, but jars of clay. We are fragile, vulnerable, even breakable pieces of pottery, which are being shaped, molded, fired in the furnace of hardship, painted and polished by the Craftsman of our souls. As jars of clay, God's all-surpassing creative power is on display in our lives.

Nothing highlights the skill of an artisan quite like working with clay. It is just clay after all, but a skilled craftsman can take what is little more than dirt and produce a beautiful work of art. Although many artisans working with gold and silver are skilled as well, much of what you note when looking at those products is simply the beauty of the materials themselves. After all, precious metals are beautiful in and of themselves, and any craftsman working with gold or silver has a leg up on those working with clay. Be honest, no one ever sees a piece of pottery and says, "Now that is a stunning piece of dirt!"

When a piece of pottery catches our eye, it is because we are stunned by the skill of the craftsman, not the materials with which they were working! No one is struck by the beauty of clay until it is shaped, glazed, fired, painted, and polished. And we are lumps of clay, meant not to draw attention to ourselves, but to display the awesome power of God's grace at work in us.

Now some of us may feel more like vessels of gold or silver than earthen vessels, because we are on top of the world. That is a great place to be, as long as we have an accurate perspective of ourselves when compared to God. It is good to feel good, unless it blurs our perspective of reality. We may be highly successful, but we are still just jars of clay. Which is not to say that we are worthless. That is certainly not Paul's point.

The treasure we possess in Jesus Christ is infinitely more valuable than anything we could ever hope to offer God in and of ourselves. Using Paul's metaphor of clay, you could say that our righteousness is like dirt, but the good news of the gospel is that God entrusts us with the treasure of Jesus Christ's righteousness in order to "show off" his all-surpassing power.

Conclusion

Disciples are those who have freely received God's gracious forgiveness and continue by the same grace as followers of Jesus. We begin and end the journey of faith based upon the grace of God and nothing else. I am sure that some feel very much like jars of clay, even after receiving God's grace, as we are often keenly aware of our flaws, and are fragile, even broken. For those of us haunted by our earthly qualities, you may be wondering whether there is really anything to feel good about in life. How do we handle our weaknesses and failures? How do we hold the reality of our own experience in one hand, while in the other hand hold out hope for the future? The good news of the gospel of Jesus Christ is that God's grace is sufficient, no matter how we may feel or what we may be facing (2 Corinthians 12:9).

Group Discussion Questions

1. How is your experience similar or dissimilar to Gordon Mac-Donald's quote found at the beginning of the chapter? (Ephesians 3:10-12)

2. Considering George Wilson's refusal of a presidential pardon, what are some of the more common reasons people refuse God's offer of forgiveness?

3. In light of the reported faith of Jeffrey Dahmer, how does it make you feel to know that God's grace is available to all without discrimination?

4. What evidence of "sin management," or of "undermining grace" do you see in your own life? Within the church?

5. If you have never prayed to receive God's forgiveness of your sin, what prevents you from doing so now?

6. If you have prayed to receive God's forgiveness of your sin, describe your experience.

7. How do you see God continuing the work of grace that he started in your life, and how patient are you with the process of his workmanship? (Ephesians 2:10, Philippians 1:6)

8. What evidence of "clay" do you see within your life, and how have you seen God use you despite your earthly qualities? (2 Corinthians 4:7)

9. How would you like people to pray for you in the days ahead, as you apply what you have learned in this chapter to your life?

Chapter 4
Charismaniacs

----

*Therefore, I urge you, brothers, in view of God's mercy,
to offer your bodies as living sacrifices, holy and pleasing
to God—this is your spiritual act of worship.*
The Apostle Paul

During my senior year of college I sold new cars at a local dealership. It is not an exaggeration to say I learned more about business at that dealership than in all my college economics classes combined. The first lesson I learned was "sell what you can see, don't see what you can sell." The dealer was not interested in ordering cars for their customers. They wanted to move the inventory on the lot, and their best strategy for doing so was the *bait and switch.*

Each Saturday morning as we were getting ready to open, the owner of the dealership looked over the advertisements in the weekend newspaper, making special note of the promotions offered at other dealerships. Our ads were in the paper too, but we seldom had the cars on the lot that we advertised. Ads went to print so early in the week that we usually sold the cars advertised before the promotions were published. This meant the ads functioned as little more than consumer "bait." It was understood that the salesmen were expected to "switch" customers from the cars featured in the ads to the cars on the lot.

The good news about discipleship is that there is no bait and switch. We are not lured into relationship with Jesus with the promise of grace and mercy only to experience law and condemnation. Both salvation (i.e. the initial experience of receiving God's forgiveness for our sin by accepting Jesus' sacrificial death on our behalf), and sanctification (i.e. the ongoing process of being transformed into Christ's image), are the result of God's gracious work in our lives.

Charismaniacs

While we are saved by faith through God's grace alone (Ephesians 2:8), our faith is not without evidence. In other words, although we cannot do anything to earn salvation, those receiving God's forgiveness cannot help but respond in God-honoring ways. Paul writes that God's grace "teaches us to say 'No' to ungodliness" (Titus 2:11-12), which means it teaches us to say "Yes" to something else. Discipleship is a life of saying yes to a lifestyle of worship.

In the Gospel of Luke we read the story of a woman who is described as sinful, but says "Yes!" to a lifestyle of worship as she pours perfume on Jesus' feet (Luke 7:36-50). Struck deeply by God's grace, she drops her normal daytime routine, walks across the village to where Jesus is eating lunch, enters someone's home uninvited, interrupts the mealtime conversation, and showers Jesus with praise. With total disregard for social and cultural expectations she bursts into the home of a stranger and gushes, quiet literally, all over the guest of honor. Receiving God's grace will always provoke a response of worship. We may worship alone, in the car or in our bedroom, but we cannot help but worship. In fact, we know that we are growing in grace when we have an increasing disregard for what others may think of our passionate expression of love for Jesus. Discipleship means passionately expressing honor for Christ, with increasing disregard for being honored by men.

I will never forget seeing the story of the sinful woman's worship play out right before my eyes. A senior pastor who was coaching me on some leadership issues invited me to sit in on one of his weekly staff meetings. I did not learn much about leadership that day, but I did learn something about discipleship and worship. Towards the end of the staff meeting, after all the administration and programming work was over, there was a short time of singing. All the staff gathered around a piano at the far end of the room, and as the music started, this guy, whom I had not met, shot to his feet and thrust both of his arms over his head. My first thought was, "I didn't realize this was a charismatic church!" But then I noticed that no one else stood.

Everyone else remained seated for the entire time of singing. Slowly though, the intensity and the passion of this guy's movements began to increase. He was already singing loudly, when he next began to sway back and forth, and make motions to the music with his hands. Of course, I was trying hard not to stare. After all, I was supposed to be singing also, focusing on Jesus, but it was like a train wreck and I could not help but look.

After the singing time was over, I immediately asked the senior pastor about the man. He just chuckled. "Yeah," he said, "I probably could have warned you that he can get pretty excited." Then the senior pastor explained that this man was once an alcoholic. His wife and children had given up on him. His family had disowned him, but he experienced God's grace and was dramatically restored. Today, this man's role on staff at the church is to hire young men from the community who are in trouble with the law, most of whom have chemical dependency problems, and expose them to God's love.

By the end of staff meeting the only person I wanted to talk to at this large and highly effective church with over 50 full-time ministry staff was their janitor. His love for God, expressed in extravagant and passionate praise, made it obvious that he had experienced God's grace at a deep level. It is true that we do not have to become ecstatic or frenzied when singing in order to worship. In fact, there are a lot of out-of-control displays of emotion that are probably dishonoring to our God. But we can expect that the more of God's grace we experience the more passionate our expression will become.

Living Outside the Box

It was common in the first century for dinner parties like the one Luke describes in chapter 7 of his Gospel to be open to the public. That is how the sinful woman in the story gained access to the house so easily. Rabbis would gather for lunch in the outer courtyard of a home, and people from the village would crowd around the edge of the courtyard to listen to the teachers' discussion during their meal.

It was highly unusual, however, for a woman to enter the court-yard, and culturally out of bounds for her to approach the table, not to mention to touch one of the men. But she was so overwhelmed by the experience of grace that social expectations did not box her in. She was going to say thanks to Jesus no matter what others thought of her. She even let her hair down, which was considered highly immodest. Women in the first-century Jewish community would never let their hair down in public. Next she begins crying, breaks open an expensive jar of perfume, and begins wiping Jesus' feet with her hair. It is a dramatic scene. And yet Jesus honored this woman's display as an act of true worship.

King David was also a passionate worshiper, unafraid of what others might say about him or do to him. Wanting to celebrate God's goodness, he decided to bring the Ark of the Covenant to Jerusalem. The Ark of the Covenant was the box that held the Ten Commandments. Bringing the Ark to Jerusalem was an important national event and no small undertaking, involving a parade with thousands of people lining the streets and tremendous pomp and circumstance (2 Samuel 6).

As the Ark enters Jerusalem everyone present recognizes it as the fulfillment of God's promises to the nation and David recognizes God's grace in his life and his response is an expression that cannot be contained. He is at the head of the parade, in front of the Ark of the Covenant, leading thousands of people and he is dancing. The Scripture says that he was dancing with "all his might, and was wearing only a linen ephod" (2 Samuel 6:15).

Make sure you have and accurate picture of the scene. The king was leading a parade in his underwear while thousands of citizens from the capital city lined the streets. David's worship was outside the box. It was extravagant and passionate, and predictably not everybody liked his show of emotion, especially his wife. When David arrived home that evening he heard about it from Michal. She criticized his behavior, labeling it as embarrassing for crown and the kingdom. David's wife accused him of "shaming himself." "Can't you act with a little more dignity? After all, you are the king!" she barked.

Thankfully, David did not cave to Michal's criticism, because God is pleased by lives filled with passionate worship. And we can expect that as the grace of God becomes more and more evident to us, our response in worship will become more and more foolish from the world's perspective. Paul clearly states that this type of sweet abandon will not be understood by unspiritual people. He writes:

> The man without the Spirit does not accept the things that come from the Spirit of God, for they are foolishness to him, and he cannot understand them, because they are spiritually discerned. 1 Corinthians 2:14 (NIV)

Abandon in a life of worship is not going to be understood by those who have not experienced God's grace, which means we cannot allow the world to define worship. The temptation in life is to spend our time navigating the path of greatest acceptance and least resistance, but in so doing we become focused on self-preservation and our purposes become self-centered. Followers of Jesus are Christ-centered, focused on honoring him, rather than looking for ways to honor themselves or others.

Hitting the Target

Discipleship is an invitation to offer our lives in worship, our bodies, minds, careers, families, friendships, and relationships. Only as we do this do we find any real purpose in life. In fact, Paul wrote that we are to offer our "bodies as living sacrifices, holy and pleasing to God," and he labeled this our "spiritual act of worship" (Romans 12:1).

One of the questions I am most often asked as a pastor is, "What is God's will for my life?" God's will is made known in the call to worship him. Worship is not just one aspect of a disciple's life. As followers of Jesus, worship *is* our purpose for living. God wants to transform every activity of our lives into an activity that brings him praise and honor, which gives us eternal purpose and meaning.

Our marriages are an opportunity to worship God, honoring him by giving our lives away to our spouses. Our careers are an opportunity to worship. Even if we are underemployed or unappreciated by our employer we can offer God a passionate expression of love by doing all that we do for God's glory (1 Corinthians 10:31). Parenting is to be an act of worship as we care for those God has entrusted to us. Yard work and housework are to be acts of worship. If you are a student, studying is to be an act of worship as we make the most of the gifts and opportunities that God has given us. Sports are an opportunity for worship as we enjoy our bodies.

Looking at the *Disciplemaking Target,* the words *Worship in Life Continually* is the second of the *8 Attributes* surrounding the bull's-eye. Worship is honoring God above all others, and disciples are those who worship in life continually. Jesus said the Father is seeking worshipers (John 4:23-24). God is seeking worshipers because he alone is worthy and because it is in our best interest. Idolatry was prohibited (Exodus 20:4) because God knows that requiring our worship is one of the ways that he can best care for us. If we worship money, we'll become greedy. If we worship sexuality, we'll become depraved. If we worship power, we'll become controlling. But when we worship God, then we become wise, pure, and alive.

An Equal and Opposite Reaction

The sinful woman's extravagant worship, pouring perform on Jesus' feet, was criticized by those with whom Jesus was eating. In an effort to explain the woman's passion, Jesus told a parable about forgiveness. At the conclusion of the parable Jesus said:

> I tell you, her many sins have been forgiven—as her great love has shown. But whoever has been forgiven little loves little.
> Luke 7:47 (NIV)

A tragic misinterpretation of this verse is that those who have fewer sins are likely to respond with less gratitude. Those Jesus was eating with may have been less sinful than the woman who poured oil on Jesus, but they failed to respond in worship not because they had fewer sins, but because they did not see their need for forgiveness.

In other words, when it comes to sin, some of us do not feel as though we have an outstanding debt before God, while others of us are keenly aware that God has offered to cancel a debt we could not possibly pay. Ultimately, Jesus wants those with whom he is eating to see their need for forgiveness.

The most important application point from this chapter is to ask God for an increased capacity to worship. Beware however, an increased capacity for worship comes only after a realization of one's sin. For example, it was only after Isaiah was struck by sinfulness that he was able to experience God's grace and respond in worship (Isaiah 6). The janitor understood clearly the depth of his sinfulness and the magnitude of God's saving grace, and he could not restrain himself in praise. Growing as a worshiper of God will always begin by recognizing our need for a sacrifice on our behalf through Jesus Christ's death on the cross. Again, it is not that some have received a greater portion of God's grace than others. Rather, it is that some understand more their need for God's grace.

Conclusion

The more of God's grace we experience, the greater our desire to honor Jesus with every part of our lives. Disciples of Jesus are those who worship him in life continually. In fact, we can expect that as the grace of God becomes more and more evident, our response in worship will become more and more foolish from the world's perspective.

Group Discussion Questions

1. If you had been eating with Jesus when the sinful woman poured perfume on him, how would you have reacted to her show of emotion? (Luke 7:36-50)

2. On a scale of one to ten, how would you rate your comfort in expressing your praise for Jesus publicly? Give some examples, whether positive or negative, that illustrate your living a life of worship.

3. Considering the sinful woman's expression (Luke 7:36-50), and King David's expression (2 Samuel 6), in what ways is your worship expression "outside the box" from an earthly perspective? (1 Corinthians 2:14)

4. What part might pride play in your resistance to a passionate expression of worship? (Psalm 95:6-9)

5. How did King David demonstrate a heart of worship even when faced with the death of his infant son, and how was his expression misunderstood? (2 Samuel 12)

6. How are you successfully offering your body as a living sacrifice to God in worship? (Romans 12:2)

7. Considering some of the examples of worship offered above, how might you more completely offer your body as a living sacrifice to God in worship? (Romans 12:1)

8. How can others pray for you this week as you grow in worship?

Chapter 5
White Knuckles

The mass of men lead lives of quiet desperation.
Henry David Thoreau

I struggled with panic attacks as a teenager. Suddenly gripped by fear, I would break into a sweat and begin trembling uncontrollably. It was as if all the adrenaline in my body was released at once, and I would shake and convulse. These episodes would last for ten or fifteen minutes, and I remember rocking back and forth and wringing my hands through my hair, while tremors moved through my body.

It is hard to admit, but these attacks were fueled by thoughts of losing my mind. I was afraid my mind would not be able to control my body—that I was going to go limp, or go rigid, or some combination of the two. I remember praying for peace and strength, and wondering, "Where's the power promised in Scripture?" I remember thinking, "I bet the first disciples didn't struggle with things like this!" But I realize now that they struggled with much worse.

Too often, we marvel at God's work *through* the first disciples, all the while forgetting about God's work *in* those same men's lives. We cannot have it both ways. Either we believe that God worked powerfully in *and* through the first disciples, or we believe that the first disciples were powerful in and of themselves.

Peter walked on water and was the first to preach the gospel publicly, with three thousand converted that day. He served as pastor of the church in Jerusalem and wrote two of the New Testament's books, not to mention being martyred for his faith. Church tradition holds that he thought himself unworthy to suffer as Christ did and insisted that he be hung upside down on his crucifix.

But Peter was also the disciple who denied the Lord three times, and not before pulling a sword in the Garden of Gethsemane and cutting off the ear of one of the high priest's servants. Jesus even called him Satan at one time, when he discouraged Jesus from giving his life. The truth is Peter struggled with much worse than panic attacks. He was a loudmouthed, hotheaded, and aggressive man who was only able to do great things for God because he was transformed by God's power.

John also did amazing things. Often referred to as the "beloved," John was the only disciple brave enough to attend Christ's crucifixion. Consequently, he was the one Jesus addressed from the cross, the one asked to care for Mary, Jesus' mother. Persecuted for his faith, John was later banished to the island jail of Patmos, a desolate island off the coast of Turkey. Yet, nowhere in his writings is there any complaining. Instead, it's on Patmos that he pens the final book in the New Testament canon, the book of Revelation.

We cannot forget though that it was also John, along with his brother James, who were together nicknamed the "Sons of Thunder." Several stories in the Gospels give us glimpses of why this nickname fit them well, like the time they encouraged Jesus to call fire from heaven to consume a city because of its residents' refusal to receive Jesus' message. Or the time they asked Jesus to guarantee them the two most prominent positions of authority in his kingdom. James and John struggled with issues much worse than panic attacks. They were self-centered, power-hungry men who consistently placed personal interests above the good of the group. Yet, they too were transformed by the power of God.

From a human perspective, James, John, and Peter did not provide a promising start for the church. Without the transforming power of God at work in their lives, I would not want these guys on my basketball team, and certainly not my elder board. But Jesus has a powerful resource for change, and one that is still offered to each of us today.

No More White Knuckles

After his resurrection, Jesus spent 40 days teaching his disciples. During that time he promised them the coming Holy Spirit.

Do not leave Jerusalem, but wait for the gift my Father promised, which you have heard me speak about. For John baptized with water, but in a few days you will be baptized with the Holy Spirit. Acts 1:4-5 (NIV)

Jesus distinguishes here between his baptism with the Holy Spirit and John's baptism with water, because it highlights the significance of Jesus' ministry. John's baptism was a public commitment to works righteousness—to try harder to honor God with your life. If a Jew had forsaken the Law, then a posture of repentance—that is confession of sin and a commitment to once again embrace the Law—was expected, and water baptism was the symbol of one's repentance. The problem was that John's baptism did not bring any real change in the person's ability to keep the Law. The repentant walked away from baptism the same as they were before being dunked.

Jesus' baptism with the Holy Spirit is categorically different, because we are changed on the inside, rather than simply soaked on the outside. The writer of Hebrews proclaims, "This is the covenant I will make with them after that time, says the Lord. I will put my laws in their hearts, and I will write them on their minds" (Hebrews 10:16). The significance of Jesus' ministry is that through the baptism of the Holy Spirit, we receive God's power within us, and the Holy Spirit transforms us from the inside out. This means the burden of change no longer rests solely upon our shoulders. John's baptism was simply an affirmation of one's willingness to remain faithful to God, but through the Holy Spirit Jesus offers us the benefit of his presence and power. John's baptism imparted no power, but simply encouraged greater discipline in keeping the Law. The gift of the Holy Spirit delivers the resurrection power of God directly to us (1 Corinthians 6:19).

This means that white-knuckling change, hanging on for dear life while sinful habits take us on a wild ride and pitting our willpower against sin's attractiveness, is no longer our best resource for change. Our best resource for lasting change is God's Holy Spirit. Discipline, no matter how effective, never reaches the root of our need for inner change. We can white-knuckle our way to sobriety or fidelity, but the desire for alcohol or the longing to flirt with someone other than our spouse will remain. Through the presence of the Holy Spirit, God changes our inner person, our hearts, our desires. The good news of Jesus' baptism in the Holy Spirit is that the root of our sinfulness is finally addressed. As the Holy Spirit changes our hearts, the desires we have for sin begin to wane and our longings for godliness and our confidence in God's goodness and sufficiency begin to increase.

For a long time I tried to overcome my panic attacks by sheer force of reason, telling myself over and over that there was nothing to be afraid of. "There is nothing to fear but fear itself," I'd chant in desperation. My attempts to manage the attacks helped some, just as twelve-step groups play a role in helping some overcome an addiction. But white-knuckling through my panic attacks fell far short of providing internal confidence. Only the Holy Spirit provided real confidence and peace, as he ministered the truth of God's living Word to my inmost being (Hebrews 4:12). My panic attacks only ended as my confidence in God's goodness was strengthened through memorizing and reciting Scripture.

Hitting the Target

After sharing their last meal together in the upper room, Jesus walked with his disciples to Gethsemane. Meandering through the streets of Jerusalem, it would have taken about 30 minutes to walk to the garden. Once outside the wall of the city they passed into a small valley, called Kidron, which is little more than a depression in the landscape. The valley is lined with ancient vineyards and the disciples probably walked single file between the neatly tended rows of grapes.

It was early spring and the new growth on the vines probably inspired Jesus to offer an object lesson. He described the connection he longs to have with each of us.

> I am the vine; you are the branches. If a man remains in me and I in him, he will bear much fruit; apart from me you can do nothing. If anyone does not remain in me, he is like a branch that is thrown away and withers; such branches are picked up, thrown into the fire and burned. If you remain in me and my words remain in you, ask whatever you wish, and it will be given you. This is to my Father's glory, that you bear much fruit, showing yourselves to be my disciples.
> John 15:5-8 (NIV)

There is obviously no closer relationship than a branch's relationship to a vine. It is an apt illustration for Jesus to use as he describes the intimacy we can have with him, one of total dependence. Remaining in Christ is a key to understanding a life of discipleship. To *remain* means to stay in fellowship with, stay connected to and dependent upon Jesus. "Remain in me," Jesus says. Don't let anything distract or discourage your dependence upon me. Remain. Don't run ahead of me in busyness or self-reliance, and don't lag behind me in apathy. Adding to the *Disciplemaking Target* we're using to illustrate a life of discipleship, *Depend On Jesus' Power Fully* is the third of the *8 Attributes* surrounding the bull's-eye. Dependence upon Jesus' Spirit as our source of power is essential to discipleship.

Of course, we all have experiences which can thwart our faith. In fact, that was the very reason Jesus stopped in the vineyard and explained the importance of remaining connected to and dependent upon him. He knows the trials that lie ahead for the disciples. The good news is that Jesus makes some promises to us if we remain connected. First and foremost, Jesus promises that we will bear much fruit.

Jesus said, "If a man remains in me and I in him, he will bear much fruit." Fruit represents any good work—any God-honoring thought, action, or attitude. It is important to note that *remaining* in Christ, not white-knuckling it, produces fruit in our lives. If this sounds mystical and otherworldly, that is because it is. In fact, if it does *not* sound mystical and otherworldly, then you are probably not understanding the nature of what it means to remain. One of the reasons people often prefer white-knuckling change rather than depending upon the Holy Spirit is that it is less mystical, more concrete, and within our control. White-knuckling change simply means trying our darndest to be a better person, while remaining in the vine means waiting patiently upon the Holy Spirit to bring change, and placing ourselves in a position that allows the Holy Spirit to do his work. God's Spirit is the life-giving presence, and it's only through his Spirit's movement and work in us that we bear any fruit at all.

Jesus' second promise is, "If you remain in me and my words remain in you, ask whatever you wish, and it will be given you." If we remain in the vine, Jesus promises us that our prayers will be answered. This obviously does not mean we will receive everything we want in life. It does mean that we will receive everything he has for us.

Inside-Out Change

After a short prayer with a couple I had never met before, the husband explained that after a decade of marriage, neither of them thought they would be able to continue. Both were recovering drug addicts, both divorced and now remarried, and both were survivors of childhood sexual abuse. Feeling completely overwhelmed, I sat quietly for a moment, trying to absorb the weight of all that had been disclosed. What could I offer these folks that they had not already heard or tried? They had done decades of individual, marital, and family counseling, and now they were sitting in my office. How could I possibly help them?

After a long and awkward silence, I sheepishly confessed, "I'm was not sure what to say." "What?" the husband blurted. "I don't have any wisdom to offer you guys," I said again. I remember their blank stares vividly, and it immediately occurred to me that the family who had referred them might have oversold my counseling abilities. "But," I quickly added, "I can pray with you, if you'd like." At that the husband's eyes rolled wildly, he guffawed, and he contemptuously asked, "Pray together?" "Yes," I said, "prayer gives God an opportunity to do what we have been unable to do ourselves." "Okay," he said, glancing at his watch. We had been together less than 20 minutes at that point, and I was sure that he was regretting coming.

We bowed our heads together and I prayed. The prayer lasted about 15 seconds and there were no lighting bolts. I simply asked God to heal their marriage. The earth did not shake and I am sure they wondered how quickly they could get out of my office. I said, "Amen," shared with them a short Scripture, and I let them know that I would be happy to pray with them again anytime. We said an awkward good-bye and I figured I would never see them again.

About three months passed before the husband called. I am sure that my surprise at hearing his voice was obvious even over the phone. He said, "Pastor, would you mind doing that prayer thing with us again?" "Sure," I said quickly, and then I asked him how things had been going in his marriage. "Well," he said, "I have been shocked at how my wife and I are more patient with one another, and the only thing I can figure is that maybe the prayer therapy worked." He said the words "prayer therapy" as if it were some new technique for healing. We set another date to get together.

When they arrived, I still sensed some skepticism. There seemed to be some hesitations for both of them so I asked them to share some more about their spiritual background. The wife shared first and described her experience of receiving Christ as Savior early in life, but then falling away from a life of discipleship during her teenage and young adult years. She was obviously eager to grow spiritually, and clearly understood the claims of the gospel. Next the husband shared that he had only ever attended church on holidays, and never really felt any need for religion. "But," he added, "it really seemed to help us to pray, so I'm willing to give it a try."

After hearing him share, it was clear that he had never prayed to receive salvation, so over the course of the next couple of minutes I shared with him the gospel and asked if he would like to first pray to receive the forgiveness of his sin. He said yes quickly, which caused his wife to burst into tears. In fact, she was bawling so hard that I stopped to ask her if everything was okay. "Yes," she said, "It's just that I've been praying for some time that he would be saved." I led the husband in prayer to receive Christ as Savior, as well as prayed for their marriage, asking God to continue to change the way they related to one another and to strengthen their commitment to one another. After I prayed, they prayed together for one another for the first time in their marriage, and they continue to pray together today.

Too often we are tempted to rely solely upon our own wisdom, and if this couple had come with lesser issues then I might never have admitted my inadequacy. I am sure I would have prayed with them and shared the Scripture, but I am afraid I would not have depended primarily upon the Holy Spirit's intervention. Clearly, unless the Holy Spirit did something for this couple they would be divorced today, and it is this type of inside-out transformation that was obvious in the lives of the first disciples. Men whose hearts were previously full of doubt and whose minds were full of thoughts of self-preservation were changed to men of faith and self-sacrifice.

For the longest time, I thought that following Jesus was primarily about discipline—the discipline needed to read my Bible and obey what it taught. Do not get me wrong, discipline is important to a life of discipleship, but I have grown to believe that following Jesus is primarily about dependence upon the Holy Spirit and only secondarily about discipline, because only the Holy Spirit can bring real and lasting change in me.

For this reason, when I have something I want to see changed in my life, I am learning not to throw more discipline and willpower at the needed change. Instead I am learning to invite the Holy Spirit to change my thoughts and desires (Romans 12:2, James 1:14), and to strengthen my faith. As the Holy Spirit works in my life I find that I no longer desire sin and I am increasingly able to honor him as a follower.

Conclusion

The power that raised Jesus Christ from the dead is available today through the Holy Spirit—power to overcome sinful habits and to experience real and lasting change. God's Spirit is the life-giving presence and power that we as branches receive through a connection to the vine, and it is only through the Holy Spirit's movement and work in and through us that we bear any fruit at all. Apart from cultivating our connection to him, we can do nothing.

Group Discussion Questions

1. What do you think Thoreau meant by, "The mass of men live lives of quiet desperation"?

2. Do you tend to idealize the disciples Peter, James, and John because of the powerful work of God *through* their lives, or can you identify the early disciples' need for God's equally powerful work *in* their lives as he transformed their hearts?

3. How have you tried to white-knuckle change in your life, and when have you relied upon the Holy Spirit to bring change?

4. What role should discipline play in discipleship (Philippians 2:12), and in a life of dependence upon the Holy Spirit?

5. What two changes would you like to see in your character, conduct, or concerns? How might you rely less upon discipline to provide change and more upon the influence of the Holy Spirit?

6. Considering the Scriptures below, what can we learn about how to remain in the vine, not to mention the value of remaining? (John 15:5-8; Psalm 119:11, Hebrews 4:12, James 5:16)

7. If someone knew how much of the Scripture you read and/or memorized weekly, what might they conclude about the importance of the Word of God in your life? (Matthew 4:4)

8. When has Scripture been used by God as a means for transforming your character, conduct, or concerns?

9. How can others pray for you as you work to apply what you have learned in this chapter?

Chapter 6
God's Minivan

----

*Just as surely as God desires to lead us to a knowledge
of genuine Christian fellowship, so surely must we be
overwhelmed by a great disillusionment with others,
with Christians in general, and, if we are fortunate,
with ourselves...* Dietrich Bonhoeffer *

Have you heard the joke about the man stranded on a deserted
island? He was alone for years, the only survivor of a shipwreck, when
out of the blue another man washes up on shore. As the two were getting to know one another, the man who had spent years alone on the
island was excitedly showing the new arrival around, pointing out all
the major landmarks. During the tour, the new arrival spotted three
huts on top of a hill far off in the distance. "What are those?" he asked
inquisitively. "Oh, that's my village!" answered the longtime island
dweller enthusiastically. "Your village?" the new arrival mused, "Why
do you need three huts?"

With great pride the man began to explain how the hut on the
left was his home, while the hut on the right was his church, and he
went into great detail about how he had diligently built both. "Come on,
I'll take you up there and you can look around." the longtime island
dweller said. "But wait!" the new arrival insisted, "What about the hut
in the middle of the three? If the hut on the left is your home and the
hut on the right is your church, then for what is the one in the middle
used?" "Oh, well ahhhhhh..." the longtime island dweller looked at the
ground and stuttered, obviously made uncomfortable by the question.
"Ahhhh, well, ahhhh," the longtime island dweller was searching for an
explanation when with obvious regret he finally admitted, "That's the
church I used to attend."

Relationships within the church are difficult, but we are often our own worst enemies. Sadly, the most common reason given for changing churches is not disagreement over doctrine or even leadership failures, but alienation in relationships. Most often, those who change churches describe feeling disconnected from others as the primary reason for making the change, which makes their decision even more confounding. We are too often like the promiscuous bachelor who moves from one relationship to another, desperately craving intimacy, but refusing to consider monogamy as a lifestyle. Instead of settling down and doing the hard work of cultivating intimacy with those in their current church, many opt instead to simply switch communities of faith—solidifying their perpetual sense of alienation, all the while promising themselves it will be different at the next church. They believe the lie that their biggest barrier to intimacy is always someone else.

Just this week, I learned that a family who had been attending our church for two years has now decided to attend another church. This will be their third church change in less than six years, and the supreme irony is that all three churches are identical in worship and preaching style, philosophy of ministry and doctrine. Other than their addresses, there are virtually no distinguishing differences between these three communities of faith. Certainly there are appropriate reasons for changing churches, but most of us are not aware of all the reasons we should stay at a church. Why might God want us to remain at a church and work out the difficulties in our relationships with one another?

Life Together

Considering the personalities of a couple of the first disciples provides an understanding for the relational work Jesus expects of his followers. For example, imagine the sparks that must have flown between Simon the Zealot and Matthew the tax collector. Zealots were a group of Jewish extremists who gave all their effort, even risking their lives, to the establishment of a nationalist political party.

60

Zealots wanted Israel to be self-governed and the occupying armies of Rome kicked out. In fact, zealots were committed to the overthrow of Roman power by any means necessary, even violence. Simon would have hated the Romans and looked for any opportunity to undermine their rule. The only people who Simon would have hated more than the Romans were Jews who collaborated with the Romans—like a tax collector.

Matthew would have been despised by the general population, as tax collectors made their living overcharging their fellow Israelites and underreporting their collections to the Roman authorities. To make matters even worse, Matthew was a "chief" tax collector, which meant that he would have been particularly good at extortion. He was at the top of the tax collector heap, which meant that he was exceptionally cunning and conniving.

Simon the Zealot and Matthew the tax collector could not have been more different. How difficult it must have been for them to be patient with one another, to bear with one another and care for each other. Yet, this will be our experience in every church we attend. The longer we are in the church the greater the probability we will wrong someone and be wronged by someone. It is impossible to be a part of a church without being discouraged at some point, because churches are filled with sinful people. One pastor compared the church to Noah's Ark, saying, "The stench inside would be unbearable if it were not for the storm outside."

God's Minivan

When I turned 16 the only vehicle available for me to drive was my mom's van. Like most American teenage boys, I wished for a truck or a sports car. Anything would have been more masculine than mom's van. Don't get me wrong, though. I never refused the van. I did not walk anywhere, but I did not show much thankfulness either. About the only good word I could say for the van was that it ran, and being a part of the church can feel a lot like driving my mom's van.

While the church may not be the car we want to drive, the church is the vehicle God has provided. Maybe we want something faster and sexier, but the church is what God has provided for a specific purpose within his plan. Paul declared,

> His intent was that now, through the church, the manifold wisdom of God should be made known to the rulers and authorities in the heavenly realms, according to his eternal purpose which he accomplished in Christ Jesus our Lord.
> Ephesians 3:10-11 (NIV)

The primary purpose of the church is not to make us feel better. The church is not a self-help community, whose goal is to provide strategies for living a more successful life. The church's purpose is not to make us happy, or to entertain us with programming, or to provide a safe community for our children, insulating them from the harsh realities of the world. Although each of these might very well be by-products of a church, the primary purpose of the church is to bring glory to God by revealing his manifold wisdom in Christ.

The church is the gathering of those committed to bearing witness to the mystery of God revealed in Jesus Christ. We do this verbally through the songs we sing together, through the ministry of God's Word in preaching, and through the celebration of new life through baptism and communion. We also display God's manifold wisdom physically as we display the effects of lives changed from selfish and self-serving to selfless and God-honoring, maintaining our unity despite the discouragements and disappointments we have with one another.

Although unimpressive in some ways, the church is the vehicle God has chosen to work through and we must be careful not to despise or reject the vehicle he has provided to carry his people. St. Augustine put it well when he said, "He cannot have God for his father who does not have the church for his mother." In other words, new life in Christ is experienced in identification with the local church.

No matter how risky connecting with others may feel and no matter how difficult maintaining that connection may be, discipleship means investing in others' lives in order to display God's manifold wisdom as a community.

Hitting the Target

The Greek word for fellowship in the New Testament is *koinonia*, which is built on a root word that means to hold things in common. Luke wrote of the first church that "all the believers met together constantly and shared everything they had" (Acts 2:44). In other words, the earliest church was not defined simply by a weekly meeting on Sunday in which they sang a few songs, listened to a sermon, and headed home. Luke wrote, "Every day they continued to meet together in the temple courts. They broke bread in their homes and ate together with glad and sincere hearts." (Acts 2:46).

Disciples are those who connect in fellowship deeply, and it is possible to attend Sunday morning worship regularly and still never really connect with anyone in a meaningful relationship. It is through our relationships with one another that we draw the strength and encouragement needed to continue on and grow in the faith. It is through our relationships with one another that we display the manifold wisdom of God to a watching world.

Adding to the *Disciplemaking Target* we're using to illustrate a life of discipleship, *Connect in Fellowship Deeply* is the fourth of the *8 Attributes* surrounding the bull's-eye. In the Old Testament book of Ecclesiastes we read:

Two are better than one, because they have a good return for their work: If one falls down, his friend can help him up. But pity the man who falls and has no one to help him up! Though one may be overpowered, two can defend themselves. A cord of three strands is not quickly broken.
Ecclesiastes 4:9-12 (NIV)

When deeply connected to others we bear more fruit, we're more likely to overcome pitfalls and avoid temptations, and we're not as easily overpowered when attacked with doubt and/or discouragement. For these reasons strong connections with other Christians are essential. In fact, without deep connections with other Christians we will not fully mature in our faith. The writer of Hebrews warns us:

> Let us not give up meeting together, as some are in the habit of doing, but let us encourage one another—and all the more as you see the Day approaching. Hebrews 10:25 (NIV)

The "Day" approaching is a direct reference to the future Day of Judgment in which all believers are called to give an account of how they spent their time, talents, and treasure. Gathering regularly with other believers between Sunday worship services helps us stay on track spiritually, and helps us avoid wasting our lives. The place where Christ is leading us, we cannot get to on our own. We must travel together. It is a part of God's design. And to really help one another prepare for the Day of Judgment will require the risk of opening up our lives and submitting to one another's input.

One of the real barriers to biblical community is the time required to cultivate these deep connections. Many insist that they simply do not have time to meet with others during the week. Some even struggle to attend Sunday worship regularly. But to say that we do not have time is not a statement of fact, but rather a statement of priorities.

I recently read the biography of a Chinese pastor who was jailed and beaten during the 1980s for sharing his faith. It was interesting to read his description of what was hardest about the persecution he endured. It was not the accusations, or the beatings, or even the electrocutions that he faced on a fairly regular basis over several years' time while in jail. The hardest part of his persecution was being separated from other believers who were a part of the house church movement. He missed the Christian community—the church.

Ironically, after being jailed for four years, the hardest part of going home was separating from the fellowship of the believers that God had provided for him while in jail. While in jail, this pastor, to the great consternation of the prison officials, had not stopped sharing his faith and many on his cellblock had accepted Christ as Savior. They had started a church in jail and he missed their encouragement in the faith.

Conclusion

Disciples connect in fellowship deeply. With whom do you share your life? Do you have a handful of believers who encourage your faith, bear your burdens, and support you along the journey? Again, it will take time and require a great deal of effort to cultivate intimacy with others. Even if you meet with believers regularly, deep connection does not come naturally or easily. In fact ever fiber in our being and in our culture pushes us out of community and so it takes an immense amount of intentional work to be the church.

Group Discussion Questions

1. To what was the early church devoted, and how should this provide direction for churches today? (Acts 2:42-47)

2. What impact should the church's purpose have upon a decision to leave or stay at a particular church? (Ephesians 3:10-11)

3. Based upon what we know of the activities of the early church and God's purpose for the church, what are some reasons (good or bad) to change churches?

4. If you are not currently meeting regularly with a small group of believers (i.e. Bible study, prayer group), why not?

5. With whom do you meet regularly for spiritual encouragement and how have you been able to strengthen one another?

6. On a scale of 1 to 10, rate the intimacy you share with your spiritual community and the effort you are making to love those who are different than you.

7. Make a list of the positive activities or attitudes that strengthen intimacy and help avoid alienation in your relationships.

8. How can you overcome any negative activities or attitudes that prevent intimacy among those with whom you meet regularly?

9. If disciples are those who connect in fellowship deeply, then how might you be able to grow "deeper" in your connection to other believers in the coming months?

10. How would you like others to pray for you as you apply what you have learned in this chapter to your life?

Chapter 7
Simon Says

----

*Most people are bothered by those passages of Scripture
they do not understand, but the passages that bother me
are those I do understand.*
Mark Twain*

In 2004 PBS produced a fascinating four-hour special titled "The Question of God." Based on a book with the same title, the content for this PBS special grew out of a course taught for over 25 years at Harvard University by Dr. Armand Nicholi. The course compares the lives and the philosophies of Sigmund Freud and C.S. Lewis.

Sigmund Freud was an atheist and a materialist who believed that there was no meaning to life outside the physical experiences of this world. His philosophy was based on what he called the "pleasure principle," which held that sexual expression was the greatest goal of life and sexual repression was humanity's chief enemy. Freud went so far as to say that outside physical pleasure, no meaning or purpose was available for mankind.

C.S. Lewis, on the other hand, was a Christian who believed in the absolute authority of the Bible and that happiness came as a by-product of disciplined living. He believed that moral relativism of the type that Freud encouraged only leads to a life of unhappiness and emptiness. The highest expression of love for Lewis came through self-sacrifice, which he believed was demonstrated most clearly in Jesus Christ's death on the cross as a sacrifice for the sins of all those who will receive his death as a substitute in their place.

One the most fascinating aspects of this PBS series was its effort to not only outline the philosophies of these men, but also to trace the outcome of their lives. This series made painfully obvious that what we believe matters, as it ultimately determines how we behave and consequently steers the entire course of our lives. Freud, by his own admission, was miserable much of his life. He had trouble establishing and maintaining friendships, was obsessed with the date of his own death, and died by physician-assisted suicide at the age of 83. Lewis, on the other hand, found great joy and deep meaning through his relationships with God and others, and faced both his own, as well as his wife's, death with great courage.

Dr. Nicholi sums up his reasons for spending 25 years studying these two men's thoughts and behaviors by saying that their views ultimately represent the two conflicted parts of every person. One part, he believes, "yearns for a relationship with the source of all joy, hope and happiness"—that is God. While another part of us "raises [our] fist in defiance," and says "I will not surrender."

Hitting the Target

Unfortunately, many Christians seem to live conflicted too, yearning for intimacy with God and at the same time refusing to live in obedience to his commands. This conflict appears to be rooted in a belief that the doctrine of salvation by grace and the call of obedience to God's Word are at odds with one another. And while many are eager to receive God's gift of forgiveness through the death of his Son, it seems many are hesitant to obediently follow Jesus' teachings. The apostle Paul links God's grace directly to a life of obedience.

> For the grace of God that brings salvation has appeared to all men. It teaches us to say "No" to ungodliness and worldly passions, and to live self-controlled, upright and godly lives in this present age. Titus 2:11-12 (NIV)

Most simply put, the more of God's grace we experience, the more obedience we will demonstrate. It is true that we are saved by grace, apart from anything we do. But we are saved for obedience. According to Scripture, disciples are those who obey Jesus' commands, which does not mean that disciples are perfect in their attitudes and actions. It does mean, however, that disciples are eager to live according to God's Word. Jesus said, "If you love me, you will obey what I command" (John 14:15). Adding to the *Disciplemaking Target,* disciples are those who *Obey Jesus' Teaching Wholly.* This is the fifth of the *8 Attributes* of a disciple.

Discipleship means obeying Jesus' teaching, just as Jesus himself modeled obedience to the Father when he prayed in Gethsemane, "Yet not as I will, but as you will" (Matthew 26:39). Jesus went to the cross out of obedience to the Father's will, and each of us must demonstrate a Gethsemane posture in life.

Storm Stories

The Weather Channel has a segment titled *Storm Stories.* Oddly, though, every storm story seems to include a couple of people who, against better judgment and all common sense, try to drive their car through high water only to nearly lose their lives. To emphasize the importance of obedience, Jesus told the first storm story.

Therefore everyone who hears these words of mine and puts them into practice is like a wise man who built his house on the rock. The rain came down, the streams rose, and the winds blew and beat against that house; yet it did not fall, because it had its foundation on the rock. But everyone who hears these words of mine and does not put them into practice is like a foolish man who built his house on sand. The rain came down, the streams rose, and the winds blew and beat against that house, and it fell with a great crash. Matthew 7:24-27 (NIV)

Successfully enduring the storms of life depends upon our willingness to obey Jesus' teaching wholly. We should not miss the fact that in this storm story both of the builders, the wise and the foolish, experience the storms of life. In other words, storms are no respecters of people. The promise is not that Christians are spared all trials, but that a life founded upon the teachings of Christ is able to endure trials.

In the summer climate of the Middle East the soil is baked by the sun and made rock hard by the intense heat. For this reason, all plots of ground appear to be equally suitable for a building site. But in the winter months, sudden and heavy rainfall, along with stiff winds, create rivers of mud that sweep through valleys carrying off everything that is not securely fastened down. A builder must take extra care in this type of climate to dig down to the rock beneath the dirt, excavating the loose sand and establishing the foundation upon an immovable object. Outside the teachings of Jesus Christ there is no lasting stability in this world and the storms of life could destroy us.

Peace in Judgment

Some believe that Jesus' parable of the wise and foolish builders is not referring to the general storms of life that are common to all, but rather to the very particular storm of God's coming judgment. Coming judgment is a prominent theme in Jesus' teaching, especially in the Sermon on the Mount, which this parable follows. Jesus had just finished telling the crowd that "Not everyone who says to me, 'Lord, Lord, will enter the kingdom of heaven, but only he who does the will of my Father who is in heaven" (Matthew 7:21). He had just taught on the mandate to forgive others, love our enemy, and store up treasures in heaven rather than on earth. He had just finished teaching that the gate is narrow that leads to life, and that a good tree bears good fruit. Then he warns the people not to build their lives upon any foundation other than his teachings.

The man who builds his house on the rock is the person who is wisely prepared for the judgment day and who will enter the kingdom of God. The man who built upon the sand is foolishly unprepared for God's judgment, and his end is destruction. The contrast of the wise and the foolish here highlights the difference between C.S. Lewis' life and Sigmund Freud's, between those who accept and obey Christ's teachings and those who do not. Ultimately, obedience to Scripture is a primary indication that we are in fact disciples, and obedience will include activities like:

- Serving others (John 13:17).
- Telling the truth (John 16:13).
- Forgiving those who hurt us (Matthew 6:14-15).
- Praying for our enemies (Matthew 5:44, Luke 6:28).
- Sharing the gospel (Matthew 28:19).
- Storing up treasure in heaven (Matthew 6:19).
- Caring for widows and orphans (James 1:27).

Paul also writes of God's judgment and uses a similar building analogy, pointing out that some Christians will suffer loss in the experience of judgment, while others will receive rewards. The outcome of our judgment depends upon how we build our spiritual house—that is, whether or not we live obediently.

By the grace God has given me, I laid a foundation as an expert builder, and someone else is building on it. But each one should be careful how he builds. For no one can lay any foundation other than the one already laid, which is Jesus Christ. If any man builds on this foundation using gold, silver, costly stones, wood, hay or straw, his work will be shown for what it is, because the Day will bring it to light. It will be revealed with fire, and the fire will test the quality of each man's work. If what he has built survives, he will receive his reward. If it is burned up, he will suffer loss; he himself will be saved, but only as one escaping through the flames. 1 Corinthians 3:10-15 (NIV)

The foundation that Paul references is faith in Jesus Christ, and Paul's point in these verses is that we should be careful how we build upon this foundation. We will each stand before God on Judgment Day and the quality of the life we lived will be evaluated. Much like fire tests the quality of a builder's work, each Christian will give an account for how they used their time, talents, and treasure.

While this is not a judgment determining where we spend eternity, but rather whether we receive rewards or suffer loss in heaven, this passage encourages Christians to build the structure of their lives with quality materials. This passage is a warning against wasting our lives. Using Paul's analogy, wasting our lives is like building a straw hut on a concrete slab. Make no mistake: what we do in this life, whether we are wise or foolish, obedient or disobedient, affects our experience in the next life. Our eternal experience is determined in part by the use of our temporal resources.

This should make us all ask, "What does it mean to build with straw rather than gold?" Paul goes on in this passage to address the use of our bodies, reminding us that our bodies are the temple of the Holy Spirit and warning believers not to misuse their bodies. Certainly the misuse of our bodies, whether sexually or otherwise, can be one way to build with poor quality materials (1 Corinthians 3:16-17). Later in this passage, Paul also talks about living according to a biblical wisdom rather than by a wisdom based upon the world's understanding. Accepting Jesus as Savior only to adopt the world's wisdom on money, power ,or position is another example of building with poor quality materials (1 Corinthians 3:18-22).

For example, possibly the single largest area of disobedience within the American church, and conversely the greatest opportunity for obedience, is storing up treasures on earth rather than heaven. Although the wealthiest church in the history of the world, Christians in America give on average only about 2.5% of their annual income to the church. Yet, 16 of the 38 parables Jesus told addressed the use of our money and how to handle our possessions, and one of out every ten verses in the Gospels deals directly with the subject of money. The Bible spends a disproportionate amount of time on finances, because there is a fundamental connection between our spiritual well-being and how we handle our money. We cannot divorce our faith and our finances, any more than we can separate our sexuality and our spirituality, or our willingness to forgive others and our wanting to be forgiven by God. Our faith and our finances are necessarily and inseparably linked. In fact, Jesus said, "You cannot serve both God and Money" (Luke 16:13).

Too many Christians insist that they cannot afford to give while they borrow more money to build an addition on their home, or buy new clothes and cars, or go out to dinner for the third time in a week. According to God's Word , we cannot afford not to give. If God does not have our money, then he does not have our heart.

If you are apathetic in your faith or discouraged spiritually, if you cannot get excited about going to church, or prayer, or sharing your faith or learning from God's Word or worshiping or serving, then do something that will change your heart. Give your money to God's church and you will begin to cut the strings that tie your heart to the worries and cares of this world (Matthew 6:21). Money is a trap for the soul and only giving it back to God frees us from its peril.

Jesus described money as one of the largest barriers to receiving eternal life (Matthew 19:24). Yet, how many Christians continue hoard their wealth, instead of funding kingdom-minded ventures? If you are not giving generously to support the ministries of the church you attend then you are being disobedient to the teachings of Christ, your life will be unstable, susceptible to destruction when storms come and you will suffer loss on Judgment Day.

Conclusion

Disciples are obedient to Jesus' teaching. While many Christians live as if the message of God's grace is at odds with the expectation of obedience, Jesus is clear that those who love him will obey him.

Group Discussion Questions

1. Considering Mark Twain's quote at the opening of this chapter, does the importance of obedience bother you?

2. Considering the short list of activities on page 71, how does your obedience to God's Word measure up? What steps can you take to improve your response to God's Word?

3. To what was the early church devoted, and how should this bear upon our obedience? (Acts 2:42-47)

4. Take ten minutes and make a short list of some of the decisions you made in the last 24 hours.

5. Considering the list of decisions you just identified, what might someone else conclude about whether you believe the Bible is God's Word?

6. Why might some Christians believe salvation by grace and obedience to God's Word are competing ideas? (John 14:15)

7. Share some of the Gethsemane moments you have had in life, where you submitted to the will of God, even through tears. (Matthew 26:39)

8. Where might you be building with straw upon the foundation of faith in Jesus Christ?

9. How can others be praying for you as you work to apply what you have learned in this chapter to your life?

Chapter 8
Finding a Towel

The matter is quite simple. The Bible is very easy to understand.
But we Christians are a bunch of scheming swindlers. We pretend
to be unable to understand it because we know very well that
the minute we understand, we are obliged to act accordingly.
Soren Kierkegaard *

Helen Dunkeld died at the age of 90 after serving in Africa as a missionary for 43 years. Setting sail for the Dark Continent at the age of 23, she arrived in Cape Town in 1939. After some training, she and her husband, Orval, moved into the Zambezi River Valley. There were no roads into the valley, which made travel inland slow and treacherous. They forged rivers and drove across fields. David Livingstone, the great explorer of Africa, was in the same valley almost 100 years prior to Helen and Orval's arrival, and said that it was the most primitive area of the entire continent.

In the Zambezi Valley Helen and Orval built a home of mud and thatch and shared the gospel while providing medical care. The first night in their new home a leopard broke into the fenced yard and killed their goats, which meant their supply of milk was gone. Over 100 miles from the nearest town, it would be a long time before the goats were replaced. Because of the distance to town, they were at unique risk any time there was an accident or medical crisis. In fact, tired of suffering with repeated cavities and toothaches out in the bush, on one of Helen's rare visits to town she asked the dentist to pull all her teeth. Not surprisingly, the first two dentists Helen asked refused, on the basis of her relative youth. She persisted and in 1959, at the age of only 43, had all her teeth removed.

This means that when she died at the age of 90, she had lived with dentures longer than she had lived with her own teeth. Imagine having all your teeth removed, in the prime of your life, so that you could more easily stay out in the bush and share the gospel with others.

Hitting the Target

Jesus said of his life, "The Son of Man did not come to be served, but to serve and to give his life as a ransom for many" (Matthew 20:28). Disciples are those committed to serving with Jesus, even if it means crossing oceans, trekking over land, enduring leopard attacks, or having their teeth removed before middle age, as Helen did. The sixth of the *8 Attributes* of a disciple is *Serving with Jesus Passionately*.

The night before his crucifixion, while preparing to share his Last Supper with the disciples in the upper room, Jesus provided a tangible demonstration of his service toward each of us by washing the disciples' feet.

> When he had finished washing their feet, he put on his clothes and returned to his place. "Do you understand what I have done for you?" he asked them. "You call me 'Teacher' and 'Lord,' and rightly so, for that is what I am. Now that I, your Lord and Teacher, have washed your feet, you also should wash one another's feet. I have set you an example that you should do as I have done for you. I tell you the truth, no servant is greater than his master, nor is a messenger greater than the one who sent him. Now that you know these things, you will be blessed if you do them." John 13:12-17 (NIV)

As disciples of Jesus Christ we are commanded to follow his example in foot washing. We are to lay aside our claim to position and power and authority and assume a posture of humble service. Paul writes that we should have the attitude of Christ who, although equal with God did not consider equality with God something to be grasped (Philippians 2:5-7). Instead of asserting his authority, Jesus served others selflessly. As disciples of Jesus, his posture should be the core of our conduct.

One of the ways we keep the command to wash others' feet is by meeting their physical needs through acts of service. We should not overspiritualize this passage and lose sight of the fact that Jesus actually scrubs the dirt off the disciples' feet. There are many basic physical needs that we can help provide for others, including food, shelter, and clothing. We also keep this command by meeting one another's spiritual needs through acts of service. In other words, we should not underspiritualize this passage either and lose sight of the fact that Jesus uses this physical activity to represent his spiritual service of dying on the cross for our sins. We serve others spiritually as we pray with and for another, as we share God's Word with others, listen to, encourage, and bear one another's burdens.

Note that John is very careful to point out that Judas Iscariot, the betrayer, is present for the foot washing. It is as if John wants us all to know that "Yes, Jesus washes even Judas' feet." All the while, Jesus knows full well that Judas will soon betray him for 30 pieces of silver. The promise of God for those who find a towel and serve with Jesus is blessings. Jesus says to his disciples, "Now that you know these things, you will be blessed if you do them" (John 13:17).

Misunderstanding the Call to Service

A young engaged couple came to the church one day asking for help in settling a disagreement. They were fighting over where to be married. She grew up attending an Episcopalian church, while he grew up attending a Methodist church, and it was clear that they were hoping our non-denominational church might serve as a happy compromise. However, when I asked them why being married in a church was important, they were unable to answer. She said, "Well, I never thought about it, really. Aren't you supposed to get married in a church? Doesn't that mean God will bless the marriage?" "No," I said. "The building has nothing to do with God blessing your life."

"It is a common misunderstanding," I admitted, "but getting married in a church, giving money to the church, teaching Sunday school weekly, or serving the poor does not obligate God to bless us. He wants something much deeper and more real than our simply trying to hold him hostage through good behavior."

I went on to explain that while each of these activities is good in and of themselves, God does not simply want our service. He wants *us*. Our role is different than the service a maid offers. While a maid might be welcome in a home, and their work appreciated, they are still not a part of the family who lives there. God invites us fully into his family. He wants to know us and be known by us, which means that a life of service is not a one-size-fits-all reality.

Discipleship is first and foremost a relationship that requires our responding to Jesus' unique call upon our lives. For example, service to Christ does not necessarily require selling all of one's possessions and giving the proceeds to the poor, although that was exactly what was required of the rich young ruler (Luke 18:22). And service to Christ does not necessarily require severing all ties with one's biological family, although it does require prioritizing our relationship with Jesus above all other relationships (Luke 14:26). Obviously, the first twelve disciples changed careers and traveled extensively, but service is not as simple as saying that that will be the case for everyone who follows after Jesus.

As disciples, we are to hold everything in our lives with an open hand, allowing Jesus the freedom to direct every aspect of our lives for his service. Discipleship is a journey, a process of getting to know our Creator and learning how we can best serve his interests.

Perseverance Needed

Demas was a trusted member of Paul's ministry team. In fact, when the team members are listed in Scripture, Demas is positioned prominently, before even Luke, who authored the Gospel of Luke and the book of Acts. Paul closes the New Testament book of Philemon writing, "Epaphras, my fellow prisoner greets you, as do Mark, Aristarchus, Demas, and Luke, my fellow laborers" (Philemon 23,24). Paul also mentions Demas in his close to the book of Colossians, saying that Luke and Demas send their greetings!

So although we do not know a lot about Demas, we do know that he was a close friend of Paul and someone who accompanied Paul on his missionary journeys, even suffering hardship with him. In other words, Demas was a significant contributor through his service. He bore fruit and was someone the other churches would have known well.

Unfortunately though, Demas took a wrong turn on his spiritual journey, a turn we all want to avoid. Sometime around 67 AD, about 34 years after Jesus was raised from the grave, Paul wrote to Timothy some sad news about Demas. He wrote, "Do your best to come to me quickly, for Demas, because he loved this world, has deserted me and has gone to Thessalonica" (2 Timothy 4:10). Demas loved this world. That is sad. We know that Paul wrote the book of 2 Timothy from a Roman prison, just before he was martyred for his faith. This means that Demas most likely abandoned Paul in his time of greatest need.

Demas' story should challenge each of us, because the love of the world can draw us all away from service. James, the half brother of Jesus, writes in chapter 4 of the book that bears his name,

> You adulterous people, don't you know that friendship with the world is hatred toward God? Anyone who chooses to be a friend of the world becomes an enemy of God.
> James 4:4 (NIV)

James labels those who are friends with the world as adulterers. James uses the most intimate relationship on earth to describe God's longing for us. This longing is like that of a jealous spouse, one who has been rejected and betrayed. How can we remain faithful and avoid friendship with the world? In the verses that precede Paul's comments about Demas' desertion, he gives us a hint.

For I am already being poured out like a drink offering, and the time has come for my departure. I have fought the good fight, I have finished the race, I have kept the faith. Now there is in store for me the crown of righteousness, which the Lord, the righteous Judge, will award to me on that day—and not only to me, but also to all who have longed for his appearing.
2 Timothy 4:6-8 (NIV)

Paul longed for Jesus' appearing. He was so focused on the return of Christ that he was able to withstand incredible suffering. What was it that drew Demas away? Was it fear that he too might be martyred if he stayed with Paul? Was it a desire to get away from the conditions in the prison? It could have been as simple as wanting a bed to sleep in or wanting decent food to eat. In any case, Demas was more concerned with this present world than he was with the world to come.

Each day we are faced with the decision to love either this world or the one to come, and we express our love through service. For example, we are daily faced with decisions like:

Will we buy a smaller house than we can afford in order to serve through giving more to God's work, or will we squeeze into a mortgage that will prevent our giving?

Will we be the same in private as we are in public, or will we only serve the interests of Christ when it can win the admiration of others?

Will we edit our speech, concerned about what others may think, or will we serve Christ's interests by boldly speaking up for the Lord?

The apostle Peter writes that we are to live as strangers, as foreigners and aliens in this world (1 Peter 2:11-12), because this world is not our home. It is interesting to note how Eugene Petersen translates Peter's words in *The Message*. He writes, "Friends, this world is not your home, so don't make yourselves cozy in it" (1 Peter 2:11). You can tell when cozy is not your goal, because your actions will seem strange to people who are making this world their home. Godliness is dramatically different from the world's mode of operation, which will often make us feel alienated and strange in how we lead our lives. For example, you may be asked...

- Why would you not lie on your resume, if you need a job?
- You mean you pay your taxes willingly, even eagerly?
- Why would you not gossip? What else is there to talk about?
- Are you going to forgive your spouse, again?

Apart from accepting our status as strangers in this world, we cannot grow spiritually. This does not mean we cannot enjoy life. It simply means that we cannot live for this life. Hating this world and being a friend of God does not mean that we have to act like Eeyore. We are not waiting for the sky to fall and saying "Woe is me!" Life is God's greatest gift and we are to enjoy it, but we are not to love life more than the Giver of life. We are not to worship the gift of life, making it our idol. We are to worship God, receiving life with thankfulness, and using our lives to serve him.

Conclusion

As disciples of Jesus Christ we are commanded to follow his example in foot washing. We are to lay aside our claim to position, power, and authority and assume a posture of humble service. As disciples, a life of service is to be the very core of our conduct, just as it was Christ's, who did not come to be served but to serve others.

Group Discussion Questions

1. How were you encouraged by reading Helen Dunkeld's story? How were you challenged?

2. Considering the gifts given by the Holy Spirit to Christians, which do you believe you possess and how are you utilizing them in service? (1 Corinthians 12:4-11, Romans 12:1-8)

3. Considering the following verses, how might Jesus be calling you to strengthen your service? (Matthew 20:28, John 13:1-17, Ephesians 2:8-10, Philippians 2:5-7)

4. How have you misunderstood the call to service in times past?

5. Why must our relationship to Christ come before our service with Christ? (Matthew 7:15-23)

6. How have you persevered in service in times past?

7. When have you chosen friendship with the world over service with Christ? (James 4:4-6)

8. Considering the questions on page 81, how does your life demonstrate a love of this world and/or a looking forward to the next? (2 Timothy 4:6-8)

9. What decisions have you made recently that demonstrate your "alien" status in this world? (1 Peter 2:11-12)

10. How can others be praying for you as you work to apply what you have learned in this chapter to your life?

Chapter 9
A Samaritan Experience

The Christian ideal has not been tried and found wanting.
It has been found difficult and left untried.
G.K. Chesterton*

In my second year of graduate school I took a spiritual formation class focusing on curriculum design and assessment. In one assignment the teacher divided the students into groups, giving each group the charge of writing a creative lesson around a biblical topic and then teaching that lesson to the class. When the day came for my group to teach, our three objectives were:

1. To have the class listen as we read them one of Jesus' parables.
2. To walk together, as a class, across campus, giving the students time and space to think about the application of the parable to their lives. Much of the instruction in the class had focused on the importance of creative teaching methods. The walk across campus was our attempt at creativity.
3. To discuss the application of the parable as a class.

As planned, after reading the parable we set out across the campus, for what was meant to be a leisurely stroll. The problem was the minute we stepped out of the classroom and into the open air a man approached our group. It was obvious he did not belong on campus. He smelled bad. His clothes were tattered and his hair was long and unkempt. The college often had problems with vagrants wandering onto campus and harassing the students by begging for money. This guy certainly fit the bill.

As one of the leaders of that evening's lesson, I had been the first out the doors, and I was no sooner through the door when he asked me for money. "No." I said politely but firmly, and moved on knowing that if I stopped to help then the whole group would be distracted from the lesson plan.

Passing him quickly I looked over my shoulder to see if he was going to speak to anyone else, and sure enough he seemed intent on begging from everyone who came out the door. One after another, he asked the entire class for money. He said he needed help with train fare, but he did not smell like he would use the money to buy a ticket.

When it became apparent to him that my classmates were not going to be easily persuaded to help, he became more insistent. "God," he said at the top of his lungs, "I thought this was supposed to be a Christian college." He even grabbed one of the men in the group by the shirtsleeve to try and hold him up, but the fellow jerked away. It was at that point that the professor stepped in. With great authority, the professor said, "Look here, you can't be begging on campus, and if you continue to bother us then I will call security." With that the beggar slipped away.

By this time we were halfway across campus and the group was completely distracted. No one was talking about the parable. It was probably the furthest thing from their mind at that point. Instead, everyone was talking about how persistent the beggar had been. I heard one woman say from the back of the group, "I'm okay with someone asking once, but to ask again and again is so rude. What does he think 'No' means anyway?" With that phrase hanging in the air we stepped back into the classroom, and directed the students to find a seat.

The class was stirred up from the episode with the beggar and we were having trouble getting them to settle down, so we thought it would be wise to begin the final phase of our lesson by rereading the parable we were to discuss. Bear in mind that this was the same parable that I had read to the class not five minutes earlier.

On one occasion an expert in the law stood up to test Jesus. "Teacher," he asked, "what must I do to inherit eternal life?" "What is written in the Law?" he replied. "How do you read it?" He answered: " 'Love the Lord your God with all your heart and with all your soul and with all your strength and with all your mind'; and, 'Love your neighbor as yourself.' " "You have answered correctly," Jesus replied. "Do this and you will live." But he wanted to justify himself, so he asked Jesus, "And who is my neighbor?" In reply Jesus said: "A man was going down from Jerusalem to Jericho, when he fell into the hands of robbers. They stripped him of his clothes, beat him and went away, leaving him half dead. A priest happened to be going down the same road, and when he saw the man, he passed by on the other side. So too, a Levite, when he came to the place and saw him, passed by on the other side. But a Samaritan, as he traveled, came where the man was; and when he saw him, he took pity on him. He went to him and bandaged his wounds, pouring on oil and wine. Then he put the man on his own donkey, took him to an inn and took care of him. The next day he took out two silver coins and gave them to the innkeeper. 'Look after him,' he said, 'and when I return, I will reimburse you for any extra expense you may have.' " "Which of these three do you think was a neighbor to the man who fell into the hands of robbers?" The expert in the law replied, "The one who had mercy on him." Jesus told him, "Go and do likewise." Luke 10:25-37 (NIV)

Hitting the Target

The topic my group had selected for our lesson was the biblical mandate to love others selflessly, and as I finished reading the parable for a second time the class was silent. It had dawned on them that the walk itself had little to do with the learning process, while the person we met along the way had everything to do with lesson. We had hired an actor to dress up as a beggar and harass the class, and no one had stopped to help. No one! In a class full of men and women committed to a life time of ministry, no one had stopped to even listen to the man's story, or try and encourage him, or to offer to pray with him.

Jesus said, "My command is this: Love each other as I have loved you" (John 15:12). According to Scripture, we are to give our lives away to others through acts of compassion and mercy, just as Christ laid his life down for us. In fact, Jesus said that it is "By this all men will know that you are my disciples, if you love one another" (John 13:35). In other words, the love demonstrated by Christ's followers will be a convincing proof for non-believers that the message of the gospel is uniquely true. *Loving Others Selflessly* adds to our *Disciplemaking Target* as the seventh of the *8 Attributes* of a disciple (page xi).

Discipleship means loving others just as we have been loved by Jesus, selflessly and sacrificially. It is Christ's love for us that motivates our love of one another. The apostle John wrote, "We love because he first loved us" (1 John 4:19). God's love for us, demonstrated on the cross, draws us out of self-seeking lifestyles and motivates us to lay our lives down for others and the more we are in touch with his sacrifice, the more we are going to be motivated to follow in his footsteps.

The million dollar question is "How?" How do we thoroughly experience the sacrificial love and care of Jesus Christ so that we are continually fueled in our love for others? Jesus said, "If you obey my commands, you will remain in my love, just as I have obeyed my Father's commands and remain in his love" (John 15:10). Too often obedience is treated as optional for Christians, but it is obedience that makes remaining in Christ's love possible. This is not to say that God's love for us changes based upon our behavior (Romans 8:28-39). God's love for us is based upon Christ's faithfulness to us, not upon our faithfulness to him. At the same time, our experience of his love is directly tied to our behavior.

Obedience draws us deeper into fellowship with God's Spirit, opening us to the Spirit's communication of God's love. Disobedience disconnects us from the Spirit and his communication of God's love. For this reason, Paul warns not to quench the Spirit (1 Thessalonians 5:19). Paul knows disobedience can put out the fire of the Spirit in our lives, while obedience can fan the Spirit's work in our lives into a consuming fire, and bathe us in the knowledge of God's love.

It is commonly thought that disobedience is fueled by doubt, but according to Jesus doubt can be caused by disobedience. In other words, it appears that disobedience can open the door to skepticism in our lives and that obedience can close that same door. This means that if you are skeptical in your faith then obedience is part of the remedy. If you doubt God's love for you or find yourself disinterested in loving others as commanded, then obedience is part of the answer.

Are you struggling to believe that God loves you? Has it been a while since you've experienced the comfort and encouragement of his Spirit's presence? Loving those we find it difficult to love makes us better able to enter the reality of his grace shown toward us.

Sodom's Sister

There is more to the sin of the cities of Sodom and Gomorrah than initially meets the eye, more than the obvious violence and sexual immorality that has historically been the focus of so much pulpit attention. In the Old Testament book of Ezekiel we glean some additional understanding of God's condemnation of these famously sinful cities, as God compares Jerusalem's sin to the sin of Sodom.

As surely as I live, declares the Sovereign LORD, your sister Sodom and her daughters never did what you and your daughters have done. Now this was the sin of your sister Sodom: She and her daughters were arrogant, overfed and unconcerned; they did not help the poor and needy. They were haughty and did detestable things before me. Therefore I did away with them as you have seen. Ezekiel 16:48-50 (NIV)

As we read of the "detestable things" done by the people of Sodom, these are most likely the violent and sexually immoral acts that have historically been associated with this city and are so readily apparent in Genesis 18-19. Although these sins are the easier ones to identify, it is important to understand that that is not all that God is condemning in Sodom's behavior. In fact, the sins of violence and homosexuality are the fruit of some much more subtle, but serious, roots of sin at work within the citizenry of these two cities, namely the sins of arrogance and selfishness.

Through Ezekiel we learn that Sodom was a wealthy city, with an "overfed" citizenry. Perhaps their wealth contributed to their arrogance. We also learn that it was a selfish city, as they were "unconcerned" about the poor. It is these roots of arrogance and selfishness that ultimately bear the fruit of violence and sexual immorality. We should not miss the fact that God condemned Sodom for much more than simply sexual immorality and violence. We must come to terms with the fact that living fat and happy, while others are suffering with their needs unmet will bring judgment upon us. On Judgment Day Jesus will say to us, "Whatever you have done for one of the least of these brothers of mine, you have done for me" (Matthew 25:31-46). As disciples, we must take seriously God's heart for the poor and ask whether we are living our lives like the people of Sodom: "arrogant, overfed and unconcerned."

Fat and Happy No More

The early church provides a good example of what it will mean to love others selflessly. Luke writes,

> There were no needy persons among them. For from time to time those who owned lands or houses sold them, brought the money from the sales and put it at the apostles' feet, and it was distributed to anyone as he had need. Acts 4:34-35 (NIV)

The point of these verses is not to encourage communal living. God is not so naïve as to suggest that fellowship is created by simply sharing property. Luke records the phenomenal generosity among the believers as an outcome, not a prescription. His point is that Christ's followers care for others selflessly.

Christians are not mandated to live in complete financial inter-dependence, but we are to live intertwined lives. The apostle Paul wrote, "Carry each other's burdens, and in this way you will fulfill the law of Christ" (Galatians 6:2). In fact, a good working definition for church is "the fellowship of those given by Christ to be to each other what he has been to them, unconditionally loving and sacrificial." The well-fed, well-clothed, well-housed, well-entertained Christians who insulate themselves from the hungry, the naked, and the homeless of the world are incompatible with the idea of discipleship.

We must stop believing that godliness is primarily the avoid-ance of certain sins and we must begin to see godliness as the pursuit of and care for the least and the lost among us. Only then will the gospel message that the church brings to the world be thoroughly convincing. When we are giving, cheerfully and sacrificially, to meet the needs of others, who can deny the supernatural presence and power of God among us? Furthermore, who can resist wanting to be a part of it?

Sadly, many Christians believe that the church would be more effective in reaching the lost if only God would do the physical mira-cles that he once did during the early church. But physical miracles are not the most convincing proof of God's power and presence among us. Jesus did miracle after miracle and they accused him of being a demon. For this reason Paul says,

> If I speak in the tongues of men and of angels, but have not love, I am only a resounding gong or a clanging cymbal. If I have the gift of prophecy and can fathom all mysteries and all knowledge, and if I have a faith that can move mountains, but have not love, I am nothing. 1 Corinthians 13:1-2 (NIV)

The most convincing proof of God's power and presence among us is something much more difficult than someone being healed, or speaking in tongues or prophesying. The most convincing proof of God's real presence among us the transformation of the human heart from selfish and self-absorbed to selfless and sacrificially loving towards others. Unfortunately, the converse of this powerful apologetic is also true. There is nothing more repulsive than a people that claims to have received the unconditional and unmerited favor of God through the selfless and sacrificial service of God's Son on the cross, and then simply hoards their wealth and resources, while others struggle to have their basic needs met.

Conclusion

Jesus said, "My command is this: Love each other as I have loved you" (John 15:12). According to Scripture, we are to give our lives away to others through acts of compassion and mercy, just as Jesus has given his life for us. God's love for us, demonstrated on the cross and experienced in salvation, will draw us out of selfish and self-seeking lifestyles and motivate us to lay our lives down for others. The good news of the gospel is that God is asking us to do only what he has already done for us, and the more we are in touch with his sacrifice on our behalf the more we are motivated to follow in his footsteps.

Group Discussion Questions

1. Considering the story of the Good Samaritan, on a scale of one to ten how would you rank yourself when it comes to showing others compassion? (Luke 10:25-37) Give examples.

2. How have you increased in your compassion for the least over the last few years? (Matthew 25:31-46)

3. What is an appropriate Christian response to beggars? How do we balance the command to give to those who ask with the responsibility to provide for our family? (Matthew 5:40-42)

4. Why is obedience to Christ's commands tied to our experiencing his love? How has your understanding of God's love grown through a life of obedience? (John 15:10)

5. How would you like to grow in your love for others in the days ahead? According to Scripture, who brings that growth? (Galatians 5:22-26)

6. Considering God's condemnation of Sodom, why should the American suburban church be concerned? (Ezekiel 16:48-50)

7. How might you get more involved in a ministry of compassion in your local community?

8. How would you like others to be praying for you as you work to apply what you have learned in this chapter?

Chapter 10
The Hounds of Heaven

I fled Him, down the nights and down the days...
From those strong Feet that followed, followed after.
Francis Thompson*

Edward Kimball pursued the lost. For this Sunday school teacher serving in a small church in Boston that meant visiting each boy in his class at home and urging him to receive God's salvation. Unable to meet with Dwight at his house, though, Mr. Kimball decided to visit him at the shoe store where he worked. On most Saturday afternoons Dwight could be found stocking shelves in the storage room of his uncle's store. It was there, after a short conversation and surrounded by tall shelves filled with boxes of shoes, Dwight Lyman Moody accepted Christ as his Savior. The year was 1855. D.L. Moody went on to become a prominent evangelist. It is estimated that he urged 100 million people to make that very same decision.

It is easy to trace the enormous impact that Edward Kimball's diligent pursuit of the lost has had upon history, as it was D.L. Moody who later led Wilbur Chapman to salvation. Chapman became a great evangelist as well, and while preaching at the Pacific Garden Mission on State Street in Chicago, his voice reached a professional baseball player with the Chicago White Stockings named Billy Sunday. The year was 1886 and soon Billy too was leading evangelistic crusades. One of Billy's crusade efforts in Charlotte, North Carolina led to the formation of a Christian Business Men's Club in 1924. Ten years later, that club held a crusade and Billy Graham accepted Christ as Savior.

Of course, the rest is history! Billy Graham went on to become the most prominent evangelist of the twentieth century, reaching hundreds of millions of people with the gospel. What a phenomenal impact one Sunday school teacher's diligent pursuit of the boys in his class has had upon the world—not to mention upon the population of heaven.*

Hitting the Target

God has always pursued sinners. In the Garden of Eden he pursued sinful Adam and Eve. They hid from him, but he came looking (Genesis 3:1-9). God also pursued Abraham, a pagan moon worshiper (Joshua 24:2), offering him a covenant relationship and providing him with land and descendants. When Abraham's descendants later rejected God, he still continued to pursue them. In fact, the biblical picture offered of God's pursuing his chosen people is that of a husband running after a wayward wife (Hosea 1:2). The apostle Paul wrote that while we were trapped in our sinfulness, Christ came and died for us (Romans 5:8). When we were thumbing our noses at him, he pursued us, giving his Son as a ransom for us.

While it's only by God's pursuit that anyone is saved from the condemnation brought by sin, he has called his people to join him in that effort. Christians are a people commissioned to join in God's pursuit of the lost. We are to "go," just as God has gone running after the lost throughout history (Matthew 28:19). The final of the *8 Attributes* in the *Disciplemaking Target* is *Pursue the Lost Intentionally*.

James Hudson Taylor understood the commission to pursue the lost and in 1853, at the age of only 21, he left his family in England and sailed around the world to a foreign nation and an unknown people. When he arrived, he shaved his head bald, except for a single patch on the back of his head that he wore in a long ponytail. He lived among those he was pursuing, wearing their clothing, eating their food and speaking their language. He read their books, studied their history and philosophies—all this despite their rejection of his message.

To make matters worse, many Christians criticized him for his methods. What he believed was a Christ like pursuit of the lost, others labeled as accommodating sin. Consequently, he lived a lonely and discouraged life—rejected by both those who shared his faith and by those who did not. But he persevered and served in China for more than 50 years. He established the China Inland Mission, which today is credited with bringing hundreds of thousands to Christ. It is thought that Taylor himself led as many as 35,000 people to Christ during his lifetime.

Whether we travel across the world or across the street, disciples are a people sent out. Whether we go to visit the children in our Sunday school class, or a nation of people we have never met, or a co-worker in the cubicle next to ours, disciples are commissioned to join God's pursuit of the lost.

Doubt about the Human Condition

Edward Kimball and Hudson Taylor shared in common the belief that people desperately need salvation. Yet, many Christians doubt the reality that people are born dead in their sins and doomed to an eternity separated from their Creator (Ephesians 2:1). We may concede that sin breaks our fellowship with God, but most are also quick to point out that they are really not all that bad a person. In other words, people have a hard time imagining God sending them to hell. We can imagine the sexually violent and the murderous being punished in hell, but it is hard to picture our neighbors and coworkers and friends and family suffering an eternal separation from God because of their sin.

The truth is though that while most have not murdered anyone, selfish attitudes, angry responses, and arrogant postures are common in all of our lives. For this reason, the Bible reminds us that "all have sinned and fall short of the glory of God" (Romans 3:23). It is true that not all sins are equal. Some sins are obviously worse than others. At the same time, all sin, no matter how trivial it might appear in our eyes, separates us from our Creator. All sin, no matter whether gossip or murder, separates us from God, who is perfect in his character. For this reason, we must avoid the temptation to compare ourselves with one another and instead accept God as the standard for righteousness.

Saul's conversion demonstrates this truth, showing us that even those who are comparatively good are at the same time in desperate need of salvation (Acts 9:1-19). Saul was well bred and well educated. Raised in ancient Tarsus, he spoke three languages (Greek, Hebrew, and Aramaic) and studied under Gamaliel, the greatest Hebrew intellect of that time. He had a passion for God's law and was committed to the traditions of his fathers. His social stature and religious training were impeccable (Philippians 3:4-6), but it was not more understanding or devotion that he needed. Saul needed forgiveness for the sin in his life.

Doubt about the Authority of Jesus

Even if we believe people are dead in their sinfulness and destined to hell apart from salvation, we may still lack a sense of urgency because of doubt in Jesus' authority. Disciples are those who have acknowledged the authority of Jesus Christ in their own lives, but many balk at going out into the world and declaring him as King to others. Many balk at believing that their neighbors and the people of other nations *must* forsake their own authority and submit to the authority of Jesus Christ in their lives. Yet the Old Testament prophet Daniel, some 600 years *before* the birth of Jesus, told of one coming with cosmic authority—that is universal and total authority.

In my vision at night I looked, and there before me was one like a son of man, coming with the clouds of heaven. He approached the Ancient of Days and was led into his presence. He was given authority, glory and sovereign power; all nations and peoples of every language worshiped him. His dominion is an everlasting dominion that will not pass away, and his kingdom is one that will never be destroyed.
Daniel 7:13-14 (NIV)

Daniel is describing the exaltation of Jesus, and his description is one of Jesus ruling over all the nations of the world. Daniel is saying that every race and language *must* answer to Jesus. Paul describes the same, with every knee bowing and every tongue confessing that Jesus Christ is Lord (Philippians 2:10-11). John paints a similar picture of Jesus high and lifted up, enthroned in the heavens, seated at the right hand of God—meaning that he alone possesses all authority (Revelation 5:9).

Many Christians buy into the false logic that Jesus might not be the answer for everyone. As if submitting to the authority of Jesus is on par with other personal decisions, like choosing where to attend college, or whether or not to join a health club or to start a business. The notion that Jesus might not be the answer for some that he is for others is to misunderstand the claims of Scripture. Matthew writes:

> Then the eleven disciples went to Galilee, to the mountain where Jesus had told them to go. When they saw him, they worshiped him; but some doubted. Then Jesus came to them and said, "All authority in heaven and on earth has been given to me. Therefore go and make disciples of all nations, baptizing them in the name of the Father and of the Son and of the Holy Spirit, and teaching them to obey everything I have commanded you. And surely I am with you always, to the very end of the age." Matthew 28:16-20 (NIV)

Seeing that some of the disciples doubted him, Jesus affirms his authority saying, "All authority in heaven and on earth has been given to me." The Bible claims that Jesus has been given *all* authority, which means that all people, not just some, are under his rule and reign. Believers who affirm this truth will not hesitate to go across the street or across town or, if God leads them, across the world, and proclaim his authority. It is only as we fully believe the claims of Christ, that he is the King of kings and the Lord of lords, that will we find ourselves pursuing others with the Good News. It is the knowledge of his authority that fuels our eagerness and confidence in sharing our faith.

Fear and Our Pursuit of the Lost

A final barrier to our pursuit of the lost is fear. Many fear they will not know what to say, or that they will be asked a difficult question and not know how to answer. Others fear they will be ridiculed or rejected or even persecuted. Jesus realized that we would be prone to fear so after he clarified the extent of his authority, he closed his earthly ministry by offering the comfort of his presence. "Surely I am with you always, to the very end of the age," Jesus said (Matthew 28:20). Wherever we go, whatever we face, whomever we talk with, Jesus is with us! The one with *all* authority has given us *all* of his presence.

When my wife and I were newlyweds, we lived in a subdivision with lots of non-Christians neighbors. Consequently, there were lots of opportunities to reach out and share our faith. I will admit that we were fearful of reaching out to people that we did not know, but we pressed through that fear and befriended a married couple who lived just a few doors down. They had just had their first child and were struggling with some job- and marriage-related issues. We wanted to encourage them and were hoping to share the gospel.

Toward that end, we invited them to several events at the church, which they attended and seemed to enjoy. We had them over to our house a few times, and tried to discuss spiritual matters as often as the opportunities presented themselves. For the most part, though, they did not seem terribly interested in talking about Jesus, and we did not feel terribly eloquent when spiritual matters did surface. After a couple of years, we both moved away from that neighborhood and we lost contact with one another, until recently when the wife called us. We were shocked to hear from her. We figured that they had forgotten about us and that our friendship had not made much of a positive impact upon them. The sole purpose of the wife's call however, was to say thanks for sharing our faith.

She talked at some length about how our simply being involved in their lives and inviting them to our church had led them to look for a similar Bible-based church in their new hometown. She shared that they are now both attending their new church regularly and both grow-ing in their faith. The wife went on and on about how thankful she was for our friendship and the constructive role we had played in helping them. My wife, Sherri, and I were stumped because we really did not feel as though we said or did anything particularly effective. I had actu-ally felt as though our relationship with them had been a missed oppor-tunity and that nothing good had come of it.

I have learned though that if we will simply step out and take a risk, Jesus will show up and reveal himself to others. It might not be immediate. In fact it may take months, or even years. But we are not called to be spectacular in sharing our faith. We are only called to be obedient. After all, it is his presence we are counting on, not our ability (John 15:5). If we will believe in his authority and obediently act on his commission to go, then we can be confident that his presence will go with us.

Conclusion

God pursues the lost and has commissioned every disciple to join him in that effort. We will increasingly share the gospel as we un-derstand that every person desperately needs salvation, that Jesus Christ has been given all authority, and that he has promised to go with us and work through us.

Group Discussion Questions

1. Reading the three stories in chapter 15 of Luke's Gospel, how do they illustrate Gods' pursuit of the lost? Which of the stories most closely resembles God's pursuit of you?

2. Whom has God used to pursue you in times past, whether leading you to salvation or simply working to encourage you spiritually?

3. How does the story of Edward Kimball's pursuit of the boys in his Sunday school class encourage you? How does this story challenge you?

4. Considering the impact Edward Kimball's pursuit of the lost has had upon the population of heaven, who might God be calling you to pursue? Make a short list of the people you believe God is calling you to reach out to with the gospel.

5. How might we apply the stories of God's pursuit in Luke 15 to our efforts to pursue the lost on a daily basis?

6. Of the three barriers to sharing your faith discussed in this chapter, with which do you most closely identify?

7. How does Paul describe the human condition and the process of salvation? (Ephesians 2:1-10)

8. How would you like others to be praying for you as you work to apply what you learned from this chapter to your life?

Part 3

The 4 Activities of a
Disciplemaking Church

How is the church to make disciples? Are potluck dinners, and ice cream socials central to the mission of Disciplemaking? There are a lot of good things that the church can do, but what is primary to the task of Disciplemaking? Part three of *Following Jesus* addresses these important questions.

Paul addresses God's purpose for the church, writing that "His intent was that now, through the church, the manifold wisdom of God should be made known" (Ephesians 3:10). Interestingly, God's purposes have not always been readily apparent. Three times in chapter three of Ephesians, Paul labels God's work through Christ as a "mystery," which is now being made known.

For so long it appeared that God's mercy was being extended only to a chosen few—that is Abraham's descendants, ethnic Israel. But from the beginning, God's intention was to bless all nations of the earth through Abraham's offspring (Genesis 18:18). Yet, for many millennia no one knew how that would happen.

When Paul finally recognized the mystery revealed in Christ he understood that God had chosen the Jews not simply for special favor, but for special service. Paul realized that the Jews had been given the Law and had been preserved as a nation in order to bring God's Savior into the world. God's purposes had never been limited to saving only the Jews, but to any that would receive his Son's sacrifice. It is the revelation of this mystery that the church is to make known.

Jesus Christ is the wisdom of God revealed and it is "through the church" that God is making this known to the world. This means the primary purpose of the church is not to make us feel better about ourselves. The church's purpose is not to make us happy, or to entertain us with programming, or to provide a safe community for our children. While these certainly might be outcomes of the church's activities, the primary purpose of the church is to bring glory to God by revealing his manifold wisdom in Jesus Christ. The church accomplishes this mission by making disciples, men and women who increasingly emulate the character, conduct, and concerns of Jesus Christ in every area of their life.

The final portion of this book, chapters 11 through 14, focuses on defining the *4 Activities* essential to Disciplemaking in the local church. While these activities are certainly not offered as exhaustive, they are offered as primary activities of a Disciplemaking church, each being integral to the Disciplemaking process as outlined in the New Testament. As we make our way through each of the *4 Activities* you will note that they are each coupled with two of the *8 Attributes*.

The *4 Activities* of a Disciplemaking Church

Proclaiming the Gospel	Restoring the Broken
Equipping Believers	Sending Out Disciples

Chapter 11
Proclaiming the Gospel

Ezra the scribe stood on a high wooden
platform built for the occasion.
Nehemiah 8:4

The purpose of the church is not to make us feel better about ourselves, or to make us happy, or to entertain us, or to provide a safe community for our children. While each of these may result from the church fulfilling its mission, the purpose of the church is to bring glory to God by revealing his manifold wisdom in Jesus Christ. Paul writes,

> His intent was that now, through the church, the manifold wisdom of God should be made known to the rulers and authorities in the heavenly realms, according to his eternal purpose which he accomplished in Christ Jesus our Lord.
> Ephesians 3:10-11 (NIV)

God's *eternal purpose* was accomplished in Jesus Christ, and God's *intent* is that through the church his manifold wisdom should be made known. The church makes known the manifold wisdom revealed in Jesus by making disciples, people who emulate Jesus' character, conduct, and concerns in every area of their life. The church makes disciples by *Proclaiming the Gospel.* After all, it is the gospel that gave birth to the church (Acts 2:36-47). It is the gospel that is the power of God for salvation (Romans 1:16). Unless the gospel is proclaimed, there is no church. Wherever the gospel is proclaimed there is a church, and as long as the gospel is proclaimed nothing will prevent the church from accomplishing its mission (Matthew 16:18).

What is the Gospel?

Gospel means "good news." The good news is that eternal life is provided for all who trust in Jesus Christ's death as a substitutionary atonement (John 3:16,36). "Substitutionary" simply means that Jesus took our place. Jesus died in the place of all who believe, absorbing God's wrath toward our sin, in order that we might escape death, the consequences of our sin (Romans 5:9). "Atonement" means to make amends. Through Jesus Christ's death the barrier, our sin, which separates us from a relationship with God, is removed and we are reconciled—that is joined together—with God (2 Corinthians 5:18). This is the good news and the reason Paul focused on preaching the cross.

Jews demand miraculous signs and Greeks look for wisdom, but we preach Christ crucified: a stumbling block to Jews and foolishness to Gentiles, but to those whom God has called, both Jews and Greeks, Christ the power of God and the wisdom of God. For the foolishness of God is wiser than man's wisdom, and the weakness of God is stronger than man's strength.
1 Corinthians 1:22-25 (NIV)

When Paul wrote that he "preaches Christ crucified," he meant that he proclaimed the gospel. Preaching Christ crucified included proclaiming 1) the reality of human sin, 2) the wrath of God toward human sin, 3) the sacrifice of Jesus to bear God's wrath toward human sin through his death on a cross, and 4) the resurrection of Jesus, through which he overcame death, the consequence of sin. Sadly, many are tempted to preach a message other than Christ crucified. Wanting to console folks in their sinfulness rather than convict them of their sinfulness, many preach human wisdom and psychotherapies by simply offering encouragement and inspiring stories. Of course, there is nothing wrong with offering encouraging stories or psychotherapy. After all, all truth is God's truth. The problem is that not all truths are equally vital, and many lesser truths are crowding out the gospel.

In fact, Paul warned his pastoral protégé, Timothy, that such would be the case—that men would want to be entertained rather than hear the desperate reality of their condemnation because of sin.

> For the time will come when men will not put up with sound doctrine. Instead, to suit their own desires, they will gather around them a great number of teachers to say what their itching ears want to hear. They will turn their ears away from the truth and turn aside to myths. 2 Timothy 4:3-4 (NIV)

Having good news to proclaim means that there must also be some bad news. Peter said, "He commanded us to preach to the people and to testify that he is the one whom God appointed as judge of the living and the dead" (Acts 10:42). Peter goes on to explain that the gospel is an invitation to escape certain judgment. The death of Christ is good news because of the certainty of judgment due to our sin!

Week after week after week, we are to preach the same message, Christ crucified. Some get bored and ask for more practical application. Yet there is nothing more practical than a growing understanding of the gospel—Jesus taking our place in death and providing us life through his resurrection. Nothing is more practical and applicable to life than the message of the gospel. Because of God's grace in Christ I can parent without fear, love my spouse unconditionally, serve my co-workers rather than compete with them, share my money generously, and discipline my body. Everything changes because of the gospel. The single most important and relevant contribution the church can make is clearly communicating the gospel.

Why Does the Gospel Need Proclaiming?

Another word for "proclaiming" is preaching. John the Baptist preached "Repent, for the kingdom of heaven is near" (Matthew 3:1-2). Jesus followed him with the same message, "preaching the good news of the kingdom," (Matthew 4:23). Preaching was the charge given to the first disciples (Matthew 10:7-8), as well as the primary tool in the early church's effort to spread the gospel. Peter explains to the people gathered in Cornelius' house, "He commanded us to preach" (Acts 10:42), and like Peter all Christians are commissioned to proclaim the good news of God's salvation (2 Corinthians 5:20).

But why does the gospel need to be proclaimed? Why doesn't God simply write the message of the gospel in the sky for everyone to see and understand? The short answer is that God has chosen to work through preaching because it brings him the greatest glory and his people the greatest joy. Preaching brings God glory and his people joy because it requires faith. It requires faith because it is an activity whose success depends solely on God's intervention in the lives of the listeners. Paul explains this truth,

> The man without the Spirit does not accept the things that come from the Spirit of God, for they are foolishness to him, and he cannot understand them, because they are spiritually discerned.
> 1 Corinthians 2:14 (NIV)

Only the Spirit of God makes spiritual truths understandable. While some speakers may be more eloquent than others, eloquence can never change the heart or mind of a person. Whether it is parents sharing Scripture with their children, or employees and bosses sharing Scripture with coworkers, or friends sharing Scripture with their neighbors, any time God's Word is spoken, faith is activated in that the outcome is determined not primarily by the eloquence of the communicator, but by God.

At the same time, the necessity of God's work in the lives of those who hear the gospel does not provide us with an excuse to preach poorly or dispassionately, or to be unprepared. In fact, we know from Scripture that we are to study diligently (2 Timothy 2:15), and to be prepared to give an answer to anyone who would ask the reason for the hope we have in Christ (1 Peter 3:15).

Instead, the necessity of God's work in the lives of those who hear the gospel provides comfort in our weakness. It is comforting to know that God's ability to save and transform people's lives is not limited by our efforts in study or the failure of our most eloquent communication. In fact, Paul said that he relied on this reality when preaching.

> When I came to you, brothers, I did not come with eloquence or superior wisdom as I proclaimed to you the testimony about God. For I resolved to know nothing while I was with you except Jesus Christ and him crucified. I came to you in weakness and fear, and with much trembling. My message and my preaching were not with wise and persuasive words, but with a demonstration of the Spirit's power, so that your faith might not rest on men's wisdom, but on God's power.
> 1 Corinthians 2:1-5 (NIV)

Anyone who faithfully proclaims God's Word, no matter how brilliant or dull their intellect, can be confident that God will work for his glory in the lives of the listeners and bring joy in the lives of the proclaimers. Look at what God says about his power to work through his Word.

> As the rain and the snow come down from heaven, and do not return to it without watering the earth and making it bud and flourish, so that it yields seed for the sower and bread for the eater, so is my word that goes out from my mouth: It will not return to me empty, but will accomplish what I desire and achieve the purpose for which I sent it.
> Isaiah 55:10-11 (NIV)

God's Word is special because he acts to perform it. In speaking God's Word we are depending upon him to intervene, accomplishing what only he can accomplish—the changing of hearts. For this reason, few activities are as supernaturally charged as *Proclaiming the Gospel*.

Hitting the Target

When we proclaim the gospel, we proclaim salvation by grace and we call all to live lives of worship. These are the first two attributes of disciple, which are explained in chapters 3 and 4. The Old Testament prophet Ezekiel's proclamation to a valley of dry bones is a good example of this activity. Israel had wandered from God into the worship of idols. They were dead spiritually and God told Ezekiel to speak his Word to their dry bones.

Then he said to me, "Prophesy to these bones and say to them, 'Dry bones, hear the word of the LORD! This is what the Sovereign LORD says to these bones: I will make breath enter you, and you will come to life. I will attach tendons to you and make flesh come upon you and cover you with skin; I will put breath in you, and you will come to life. Then you will know that I am the LORD.'" Ezekiel 37:4-6 (NIV)

Are the words that come out of our mouth words of faith, based upon God's truth? For example, what do we say about our ability to resist sin? Do we say, "I'm never going to beat that addiction!"? Or do we say, "I can do everything through Christ, who gives me strength"? (Philippians 4:13). What do we say about our marriage? Do we say that we are destined to live distant from our spouse, or do we proclaim that the "two have become one" (Matthew 19:5), and that our marriage will be a living illustration of Christ's unity with the church? (Ephesians 5:31-32). What do we say about our finances? Do we proclaim that "God will supply all your needs according to His riches in glory in Christ Jesus"? (Philippians 4:19). What do we say about illness? Do we say we are destined to suffer purposelessly and without hope? Or do we say that "Our present sufferings are not worth comparing with the glory that will be revealed in us"? (Romans 8:18). Do we pray for healing, as we are told to do (James 5:14), believing that his grace is sufficient? (2 Corinthians 12:9).

Do we say we will never amount to anything? Or do we proclaim that "We are God's workmanship, created in Christ Jesus to do good works"? (Ephesians 2:10). What do we say about our wellbeing and our strength? Do we say that we will always be damaged goods and broken emotionally? Or do we say, "God heals the brokenhearted and binds up their wounds"? (Psalm 147:3).

Proclaiming God's Word may sound like little more than the power of positive thinking to some. And it is true that believing God can help us overcome sinful behavior is more positive than believing we are doomed to live addicted. But we are encouraged to proclaim God's Word not simply in the *hope* that something good will happen. This is not a brainwashing exercise, although those who regularly quote God's Word do have their patterns of thinking changed (Romans 12:2). We are encouraged to proclaim the truth of God's Word because there is objective power in doing so.

Not that proclaiming God's Word is like casting a spell. This is not some type of unique sorcery. The power comes from the person of God himself, as God hears his Word proclaimed and acts to perform it. In other words, we do not control God by quoting his Word. Quoting God's Word allows God to have greater control of us and our circumstances. Proclaiming God's Word opens the door for God to work in the lives of all listening. This is part of what Paul meant when he wrote that "faith comes by hearing the Word of God." (Romans 10:17) When we hear God's Word he has a unique opportunity to give the hearers the ability to believe, which is the first step in bringing him glory and enjoying him forever.

Conclusion

The gospel is the good news of Jesus' substitutionary death. The activity of proclaiming the gospel is essential to Disciplemaking because God has ordained preaching as a means to faith. Preaching allows God to move in people's hearts in ways that only he can and results in him receiving the glory, as people believe and are saved.

Group Discussion Questions

1. Considering Paul's description of the purpose of the church in Ephesians 3:10-11, how should we identify the "essential" activities of the church?

2. How does it make you feel to learn that the primary purpose of the church is not to make us feel better about ourselves, or to make us happy, or to entertain us with programming, or to provide a safe community for our children, insulating them from the harsh realities of the world?

3. What is the gospel and what passage/s of Scripture would you use to explain the gospel to someone?

4. Why is it important for God's people to understand that "not all truths are equally vital," and what truths of lesser importance are crowding out the gospel in the contemporary church?

5. Why does sharing God's Word require faith, and what effect has the proclamation of Scripture had on yourself and others? (Isaiah 55:10-11, 1 Corinthians 2:14)

6. When and where would you like to demonstrate greater faith in proclaiming Scripture?

7. How can others pray for you this week as you begin applying what you have learned in life?

8. How can you pray for your church's effort in *Proclaiming the Gospel*?

Chapter 12
Restoring the Broken

And they brought to him all who were ill, those suffering
with various diseases and pains, demoniacs, epileptics,
paralytics; and he healed them.
Matthew 4:24

The Christian community was rocked in 2006 by yet another spectacular failure on the part of its leadership. Ted Haggard, then President of the National Association of Evangelicals and senior pastor of the giant New Life Community Church in Colorado Springs, admitted to both purchasing illegal drugs as well as a lifelong struggle with sexually immorality.

This type of announcement is all too frequent, as Christians have a tendency to pretend they have no sinful struggles. This particular scandal was made especially difficult for the church in that Pastor Haggard initially denied the allegations, and finally admitted the truth after the press published interviews with the male prostitute whom Pastor Haggard had employed.

While these types of scandals are always shocking, the truth is that we should expect this type of outing, in that it is a part of the Holy Spirit's role in our lives. Jesus said of the Holy Spirit, "When he comes, he will convict the world of guilt in regard to sin and righteousness and judgment" (John 16:8). We are all made to face our sinfulness by the Holy Spirit, whether publicly like Pastor Haggard or on a more limited and private scale among family or friends. The question is, "How are Christians to respond to sin in their life and in other's lives?" What should be the church's reaction, and plan of action, in dealing with the brokenness among its membership?

Restoring the Broken

The Old Testament book of Ezra recounts the story of God restoring the Israelites to the Promised Land. God had initially judged the sinfulness of his people, by allowing them to be deported from the Promised Land, carried off to Babylonian captivity for 70 years. Unfortunately, once the Israelites were back in their homeland they fell again into sin, and the book of Ezra is named after the priest who leads them in confession of their sin and prayer for God's restoration.

But then the Jewish leaders came to me [Ezra] and said, "Many of the people of Israel, and even some of the priests and Levites, have not kept themselves separate from the other peoples living in the land. They have taken up the detestable practices of the Canaanites, Hittites, Perizzites, Jebusites, Ammonites, Mobites, Egyptians, and Amorites. For the men of Israel have married women from these people and have taken them as wives for their sons. So the holy race has become polluted by these mixed marriages. To make matters worse, the officials and leaders are some of the worst offenders." When I heard this, I tore my cloak and my shirt, pulled hair from my head and beard, and sat down utterly shocked. Then all who trembled at the words of the God of Israel came and sat with me because of this outrage committed by the returned exiles. And I sat there utterly appalled until the time of the evening sacrifice.
Ezra 9:1-4 (NLT)

Intermarriage with other nations was against God's law, not because God hated other nations and was trying to cultivate and elite race of people (Deuteronomy 7:1-4). Truth be known, the Hebrews were from the same Semitic lineage as their neighbors, which means intermarrying would not have diluted the Jewish race. Instead intermarriage was prohibited because of the impact God knew that it would have upon the faithfulness of the Hebrews in worship.

111

God knew that the Israelites' willingness to intermarry with pagan peoples was symptomatic of their sinful disposition toward worshiping idols. God knew that if his people were willing to join themselves to idolaters in the most intimate of human relationships—that of marriage—then they would most likely be willing to worship their spouses' idols as well. And God was right. That was exactly what happened. Marriage to non-Hebrews led Israel into idolatry.

When Ezra heard that the people had not simply intermarried but that they had adopted the "detestable practices" of these other nations, he tore his clothing as well as his hair. He sat down, and the Scripture says that "all who trembled at the words of the God of Israel" sat beside him until evening. With his clothes torn and with his own hair in hands, Ezra sat appalled for hours, devastated by the news of sin in the community of God. His next movement was telling, though. He went to his knees in prayer.

> At the time of the sacrifice, I stood up from where I had sat in mourning with my clothes torn. I fell to my knees and lifted my hands to the LORD my God. I prayed, "O my God, I am utterly ashamed; I blush to lift up my face to you. For our sins are piled higher than our heads, and our guilt has reached to the heavens." Ezra 9:5-6 (NLT)

The biblical response when confronted with our sinfulness is confession, followed by prayer for God's restoration. Those who came to Ezra did not deny their sinfulness. They did not excuse their sinfulness, and they did not try and explain their sinfulness. Instead they reported rather matter-of-factly, not only have we intermarried with the pagan nations after returning from exile, but we have also adopted their detestable ways and our leaders are the worst offenders. This would not have been easy for the people of Israel to admit. After all, this was the very reason that God had allowed the people to be carried into captivity in the first place, some 120 years prior.

This type of experience is not uncommon among God's people. Sin can be much like a revolving door. We can put it aside for a while, only to pick it up again later. If you have this type of revolving sin in your life, then you know how difficult it can be to confess failure again, and again, and again. But without a full confession restoration is impossible. At best, partial confession leads to only partial restoration.

In Ted Haggard's case, it was his partial confession that led the governing board of his church to decide to remove him from ministry. To paraphrase the board's position as recorded in the New York Times, "We [finally] saw the other side of Ted, as he only confessed what he was forced to admit...and it helped us realize that dismissal was all that was possible at this point." (NYT/Nation/11.19.06)

King David said of sin: "When I kept silent, my bones wasted away through my groaning all day long" (Psalm 32:3). Before being confronted by the prophet Nathan, David hid his adulterous relationship with Bathsheba, as well as his involvement in the murder of her husband, Uriah, for nine months. For nine months he acted like nothing was wrong. After confessing he later described the damage done by denial. When we confess our sin we must make a full confession or we prevent the Lord's restoration in our lives.

After confession comes prayer. In prayer we recognize the certainty of God's coming judgment and the utter necessity of God's grace if we are to experience restoration. Ezra prays,

We are again breaking your commands and intermarrying with people who do these detestable things. Won't your anger be enough to destroy us, so that even this little remnant no longer survives? O LORD, God of Israel, you are just. We come be fore you in our guilt as nothing but an escaped remnant, though in such a condition none of us can stand in your presence."
Ezra 9:14-15 (NLT)

Ezra's response to the people's confession is complete devastation. He rends his clothes and tears out his hair, and while we may not express brokenness this way anymore, our prayer life can certainly be a telltale indication as to whether or not we understand the weight of our sinfulness. Weeping and lying facedown on the ground, Ezra's prayer of repentance highlights some realities that all people must face concerning their sinfulness, namely the certainty of, and justice in, God's judgment, as well as the utter necessity of God's grace. The good news of the gospel is that God's grace and restoration comes through Jesus Christ to all those who confess.

> If we confess our sins, he is faithful and just and will forgive us
> our sins and purify us from all unrighteousness.
> 1 John 1:9 (NIV)

God longs to purify us from unrighteousness. The commitment to restore is corollary of God's own character. If we confess, his faithfulness kicks into gear and begins the work of cleansing us from all unrighteousness and restoring our broken lives.

Hitting the Target

In the beginning God said, "Let us make man in our image" (Genesis 1:26). But when sin entered the world we lost our capacity to be the image bearers God intended. Fully reflecting his righteous character is now outside our reach because of sin, and we find ourselves broken and in need of restoration. The good news is restoration can be experienced through the ministry of Jesus Christ. Jesus said of himself,

> The Spirit of the Lord is on me, because he has anointed me to
> preach good news to the poor. He has sent me to proclaim freedom for the prisoners and recovery of sight for the blind, to
> release the oppressed, to proclaim the year of the Lord's favor.
> Luke 4:18-19 (NIV)

We live in the year of the Lord's favor! Jesus' provided hope and release to those captive to sin and oppressed by evil spirits. He healed every disease (Matthew 4:17,23), and commissioned the twelve disciples to do the same.

> As you go, preach this message: "The kingdom of heaven is near." Heal the sick, raise the dead, cleanse those who have leprosy, drive out demons. Freely you have received, freely give. Matthew 10:6-8 (NIV)

God's goal in restoration is that we would be holy, just as he is holy (1 Peter 1:16). In this process of restoration things we once had no interest in, and no desire to experience, often become attractive. We grow to desire sobriety rather than drunkenness, honesty rather than dishonesty, modesty and fidelity rather than immodesty and promiscuity. Paul writes, "If anyone is in Christ, he is a new creation" (2 Corinthians 5:17), which describes the beginning of the process of being restored as image bearers.

Restoring the Broken is an essential activity of Disciplemaking. We are all sinners and in need of repair, and we are restored as we *Depend on Jesus' Power Fully* and *Connect in Fellowship Deeply*. These are the third and fourth attributes of a disciple, which are described in chapters 5 and 6. We depend upon Jesus' power through activities such as prayer, and we connect in fellowship deeply through activities such as confession. God's design is that the members of his church would help to restore one another. Paul wrote, "Brothers, if someone is caught in a sin, you who are spiritual should restore him gently" (Galatians 6:1). Being the church of God's design means helping one another become God's image bearers once again.

A Story of Restoration

Kent and Susan met at work, dated for a short time, and were married and became parents in only 16 months' time. As might be expected in such a quick courtship, their first years were difficult. Susan often felt controlled and devalued in the relationship, while Kent often felt disrespected and burdened by the responsibilities of fatherhood.

Today, after years of turmoil, Susan admits giving up on the marriage and consciously looking for affection from another man, while Kent admits to being neglectful and verbally abusive toward Susan. To make matters worse, Susan's decision to commit adultery led to her bearing a child with another man. Not surprisingly, Kent filed for divorce. The consequences of their sins were mounting quickly and it seemed there was little hope for restoration.

Broken by her sinfulness Susan finally realized "The more I tried to make my sin okay, the more conviction I received from the Holy Spirit that it was not okay." She needed to confess and forsake her sin, rather then rationalize and excuse it. At the same time, God was working in Kent's heart and he began to realize that "Rather than turning to God in prayer, I decided to take matters into my own hands – filing for divorce and becoming even more controlling, especially with the children." Here is the story of restoration in their own words. Note the role of confession in prayer in the process of restoration.

Susan: *One Sunday morning I left for church without the kids, who were sobbing because they wanted to come with me. But something moved that morning in Kent's heart and he came with the kids to find me. By no coincidence there was a testimony in church that day of a woman who had an affair and God had restored her. Her testimony touched me so much that I asked Kent to come down front after the service to pray with the pastor. That day we both committed to stop the divorce procedure and work on our marriage. It was not all uphill from there. But it was a daily struggle. It took years. It took lots of counseling and the care of other Christians. The Holy Spirit used many people in our lives. There were many days that I would question what we were doing and it seemed hopeless but we continued on. Watching the movie* Facing the Giants *was a significant turning point for me. I was convicted by some of the Scripture in the movie. I cried out to God in prayer ask-ing for forgiveness and truly confessing my sin. I meditated on his Word and began praying for God's healing in our marriage.*

Kent: *Prayer was a major factor in saving our marriage. Prayers of our own and the multitude of prayers for us by numerous people. There is power in public confession, which led to people holding each of us accountable for our actions. We were blessed to have a couple in our neighborhood who were willing to walk through the struggle with us giving us biblical counsel through it all. They were not afraid to con-front both of us on our actions.*

Susan: *I prayed for God to give me the desire to make my marriage work because at that time I felt convicted but did not believe God could heal us or really even want God to heal us. There were days that all I could do was cry out to God in pain and cling to his Word. There were days of prayer and fasting. Ultimately we clung to the hope that if we were obedient to God he would bless us. God has answered our prayers. He has given us the desire for one another and our marriage. We are no longer together because it is right but because we want to be together. We are more in love now and are communicating better than ever before. We have seen a miracle in our lives. We have seen prayers answered and our broken lives restored.*

Conclusion

Restoring the Broken is an essential activity of a Disciplemak-ing church. The goal in restoration is that we would be holy, just as God is holy (1 Peter 1:16). Restoration comes as we depend on Jesus' power and connect with other believers. Paul wrote, "Carry each other's burdens, and in this way you will fulfill the law of Christ" (Galatians 6:2).

Group Discussion Questions

1. Considering the quote at the beginning of this chapter, why do you believe healing was an essential part of Jesus' ministry? (Matthew 4:24, Matthew 10:6-8)

2. Would you have any reservations about being a part of a church that is actively involved in restoration? Why or why not?

3. Considering Ezra's confession and prayer for restoration, when have you known this level of brokenness? (Ezra 9:5-6)

4. In what areas have you experienced God's restoration? Or, in what areas has your family experienced God's restoration?

5. To whom do you confess your sinfulness and with whom do you pray for restoration?

6. What reservations, if any, do you have to regular confession of sins and prayer for restoration?

7. What in your life, or in the lives of your family, needs God's restoration?

8. How do you see God at work through the ministries of your church restoring people to bear his image?

9. How can others pray for you this week as you apply what you have learned in this chapter to your life?

10. How can you be praying for your church's efforts in restoring the broken?

Chapter 13
Equipping The Believer

He gave some as apostles, and some as prophets, and some
as evangelists, and some as pastors and teachers,
for the equipping of the saints for the work of service.
Ephesians 4:11-12

My first gallbladder attack was the week of Thanksgiving. We were visiting my mother-in-law and I had done my duty, eating some of everything on the table at Thanksgiving dinner. About four hours later though, the pain started. It felt like someone was trying to pry my ribs open with a knife. The pain was so intense I could not stand. It lasted for about 20 minutes and then mysteriously left as quickly as it came. Unaware of the cause and afraid it would return, I made an appointment to see my doctor when we got home after Thanksgiving.

The morning of my doctor's appointment I had a huge omelet, with bacon and cheese, unaware that gallbladder attacks are tied directly to eating fatty foods. My mother was in town visiting for the Thanksgiving holiday and decided to go with me to the doctor appointment, figuring it would just be a quick checkup and we could go out for coffee together afterward. It was no routine appointment, though.

My stomach started hurting while I was in the examination room with the nurse. She was taking my blood pressure, when I started sweating bullets. The pain was so bad that I crumpled into a ball on the floor. The nurse left me on the floor and went to find the doctor. When the doctor came in I was curled in a ball on the floor and could not stand. She took one look at me and asked me what I had eaten for breakfast. Hearing about the bacon and cheese omelet menu, she quickly diagnosed me as having gallstones and suggested that I go to the ER immediately and asked if I would like her to call an ambulance.

"An ambulance!" I responded indignantly. "Well," she said, "I don't think you're in any condition to drive." Then she added, "Unless of course someone came with you this morning." "Ahh," I stammered, "my mom is in the waiting room." "Your mom?" the doctor asked, unable to hide her surprise. By her tone I could tell she was thinking that gallstones were probably the least of my problems. The next thing I heard was the doctor's voice calling out loudly in the waiting room. "Is Kelly Brady's mom here?" I felt like I was 12, but the pain in my stomach silenced the embarrassment I felt.

One week later I had my gallbladder removed. I offer this story because Paul describes the church as a body, each of us playing a vital role in God's work (Romans 12:4-5). Unfortunately, too many Christians think of themselves much like a gallbladder. Expendable.

Gifts for Service

Every Christian has been supernaturally endowed by God with a gift/s and is called by God to use that gift/s in service. Paul wrote, "To one there is given through the Spirit a message of wisdom, to another a message of knowledge by means of the same Spirit " (1 Corinthians 12:8). No one is expendable. Paul wrote,

> Yes, there are many parts, but only one body. The eye can never say to the hand, "I don't need you." The head can't say to the feet, "I don't need you." In fact, some parts of the body that seem weakest and least important are actually the most necessary. 1 Corinthians 12:20-22 (NLT)

Ever feel expendable? The Bible teaches that everyone is needed. Everyone has a gift to contribute. This means that while we thank God for those who can preach and lead worship, we should also thank God for the countless numbers who will never step onto a public platform and quietly serve behind the scenes. No one is expendable.

While it is true that when those who serve behind the scenes are most effective, no one usually knows they are there. However, if these servants fail to do their job, it is painful. It is a lot like having gallstones. Nursery workers who clean and sanitize the nursery toys between Sunday services, and the offering counters who tally the money given each Sunday, and "pew-stuffers" who clean the worship center and straighten the pens and pencils in the pew racks, are just a few examples. If these servants fail to do their jobs well, then our nurseries become germ-infested and our babies get sick, and our money is mishandled and our programs flounder, and the worship center is a mess and we are distracted on Sunday morning from giving glory to God.

It is true that we could do without the function some of these servants play, much like we can do without a gallbladder. After all, we could remove toys from the nursery altogether, or we could pay someone to count the money and clean the worship center. But the human body was designed to operate most effectively with a gallbladder, just as the church was designed to operate most effectively with everyone serving a role. To this day, I have to be careful what I eat at holiday meals, as the role of the gallbladder is to help digest fatty foods. In other words, there will always be vital roles of ministry that happen behind the scenes, and everyone is needed for the church to work most effectively. We are each to find our place of service within the church.

Equipping the Believer

Paul, in his letter to the Ephesians, outlines the importance of equipping believers for service, as well as identifying the positive outcomes for those who are thoroughly equipped.

And He gave some as apostles, and some as prophets, and some as evangelists, and some as pastors and teachers, for the equipping of the saints for the work of service, to the building up of the body of Christ; until we all attain to the unity of the faith, and of the knowledge of the Son of God, to a mature man,

to the measure of the stature which belongs to the fullness of Christ. As a result, we are no longer to be children, tossed here and there by waves and carried about by every wind of doctrine, by the trickery of men, by craftiness in deceitful scheming; but speaking the truth in love, we are to grow up in all aspects into Him who is the head, even Christ.
Ephesians 4:11-15 (NASB)

Those who are equipped find their place of service, but they also mature, no longer being "tossed here and there by waves and carried about by every wind of doctrine." It is this need for and experience of maturing that makes equipping believers so vital to Disciplemaking.

The goal of equipping is that we "are no longer children." Children are immature and are easily influenced by others. In fact, they are dependent upon others to care for them, to feed and clothe them. And while it is understandable that we would all be immature in our faith for a time, Paul's point is that we ought not remain as children. The writer of Hebrews echoes Paul, writing, "Let us leave the elementary teachings about Christ and go on to maturity" (Hebrews 6:1).

Spiritual maturity is defined not only as the ability to bear fruit through service, but also the ability to distinguish right from wrong. The spiritually mature are no longer tossed "by waves and carried about by every wind of doctrine, by the trickery of men, by craftiness in deceitful scheming," because they can distinguish between good and evil. In Hebrews we learn that "solid food is for the mature, who by constant use have trained themselves to distinguish good from evil" (Hebrews 5:13). In other words, the mature when bombarded on all sides with competing ideas, can identify and will embrace the truth.

Are we uncertain about what to believe or how to respond to the failures of Christian leaders? Perhaps the theory of evolution and not knowing how to integrate the fossil record with the biblical account of creation causes you to be tossed. Maybe the exclusivity of the gospel, and wrestling with the eternal condemnation of sincere and moral folks who reject Jesus, causes you to be tossed. Or, maybe it is not the exclusivity of the gospel, but rather the plurality of denominationalism and the doctrinal disagreement between well-meaning Christians that is difficult for you to process.

Whatever our issues or questions, we are not to settle into a passive posture of developmental apathy. We are to do the hard work of study in order to be able to distinguish between right and wrong and enjoy the stability brought by maturity. Too many Christians live in a perpetual state of seasickness, having just enough truth to avoid losing their faith but not enough truth to be fully functional. This is one of the reasons I will not go on a cruise. I am not afraid the boat will sink or that I will fall overboard. My fear is spending my entire vacation green from motion sickness.

Unfortunately this is the experience of many Christians. Many Christians are not in jeopardy of being tossed out of the boat of faith, but they are not grounded enough to enjoy the ride. Too many Christians are tossed just enough to stay perpetually seasick. That's why Paul wrote to the young pastor Timothy,

> Do your best to present yourself to God as one approved, a workman who does not need to be ashamed and who correctly handles the word of truth. 2 Timothy 2:15 (NIV)

Unable to correctly handle the word of truth and distinguish good from evil, too many Christians are negatively affected by teachings that are contrary to the plainest reading of the Scripture. Jesus said, "If you hold to my teaching, you are really my disciples. Then you will know the truth, and the truth will set you free" (John 8:31-32).

Make no mistake, Paul does not have in mind some vague notion of truth. He writes that stability is brought through a "knowledge of the Son of God...to the measure of the stature which belongs to the fullness of Christ" (Ephesians 4:13). Only when we settle in our minds once and for all that Jesus is the truth (John 14:6) will the seas of our life grow calm. But as long as we give half-hearted assent to Jesus, we will live life at best seasick or at worst tossed overboard.

Hitting the Target

Few visuals better represent the depth of Jesus' obedience and service than his kneeling to wash the disciples' feet. Washing his disciple's feet was a living parable, identifying his ultimate obedience and service through his death on the cross. Jesus said, "Now that I, your Lord and Teacher, have washed your feet, you also should wash one another's feet." (John 13:14), and equipping the saints to emulate Jesus' obedience and service is at the heart of Disciplemaking.

We all have gift/s that we are to use in service and we are each to obey Jesus' teaching. For this reason, the equipping efforts of the church focus on helping people *Obey Jesus' Teaching Wholly* and *Serve with Jesus Passionately*. These are the fifth and sixth attributes of a disciple, which are described in chapters 7 and 8 and the primary focus of the church's equipping efforts. God has provided for the equipping of all believers through the gifts that he has given to the church. Paul writes:

> It was he who gave some to be apostles, some to be prophets, some to be evangelists, and some to be pastors and teachers, to prepare God's people for works of service, so that the body of Christ may be built up until we all reach unity in the faith and in the knowledge of the Son of God and become mature, attaining to the whole measure of the fullness of Christ.
> Ephesians 4:11-13 (NIV)

The word translated as "prepare" in this verse is the Greek word *katartismon*, which comes from a verb meaning "to repair". This verb is used to describe activities like setting a bone in surgery or putting a joint back into place. In the New Testament, it is used in Mark 1:19 to describe the mending of fishing nets, and in Galatians 6:1 it is used to describe the process of restoring someone caught in sin.

The picture Paul wants to provide here is of people using their spiritual gifts in order to strengthen one another for lives of obedience and service. In some cases that will simply involve instruction, and that particular function is the responsibility of those given the gift of teaching. In other cases preparation will involve correction and even healing, which might involve people with the gift of mercy or faith. But the goal is that the people of God are ready and able to live lives of obedience and find their place of service through preparation we offer one another.

Once people obediently find their place of service, the use of their gifts is to have a very particular outcome. Paul writes in Ephesians 4:12 that God has given gifts "so that the body of Christ may be built up," or enabled. Our gifts are to add strength to one another's lives, and families. In fact, all the gifts are always given for the greater good of God's people, which is why it is so offensive when someone uses their gifts to empower or enrich themselves. God's gifts are also to produce in us maturity. Paul writes, "Then we will no longer be infants, tossed back and forth...blown here and there by every wind of teaching" (Ephesians 4:14). Immaturity brings instability in our lives, and it is our responsibility to help one another build our lives upon the sure footing of God's Word.

Conclusion

Equipping Believers is an essential activity of a Disciplemaking church. Through the ministries of the church, Christians are to be equipped to obey Jesus' teaching and serve fruitfully.

Group Discussion Questions

1. How have you trained yourself to distinguish good from evil? (Hebrews 5:13-14)

2. What are your gifts and/or talents and how are you employing them for the "common good"? (1 Corinthians 12:8) If you are not currently utilizing your gifts in service, why not?

3. What contemporary cultural issues/teachings cause you to feel tossed in your faith? (Ephesians 4:14)

4. On a scale of 1 to 10, how important do you believe doctrine to be to the stability of your faith?

5. How comfortable are you discussing doctrine and what doctrinal issues do you feel you need/want greater clarity on?

6. How have you felt "set free" by the truth of God's Word in the last twelve months? (John 8:32)

7. How would you like to be better equipped in obedience or service?

8. In what ways and at what times do you "present yourself to God as one approved, a workman who does not need to be ashamed and who correctly handles the word of truth"? (2 Timothy 2:15)

9. How would you like others to be praying for you as you apply what you have learned from this chapter?

10. How can you be praying for your church in their effort to equip believers?

Chapter 14
Sending Out Disciples

---

*You will receive power when the Holy Spirit has come upon you;
and you shall be My witnesses.* Acts 1:8

Imagine selecting the first disciples. Knowing the trials they would face and the vital role they would play in history, how would you have discriminated between applicants? What background, education, aptitudes, and psychological health would you have thought important in the success of the church?

Considering the character of the first disciples, placing them on the same basketball team would seem questionable in many respects, while charging them with leading the church seems altogether foolish. Simon Peter was given to fits of rage and capable of violence. James and John, the sons of Zebedee, were self-absorbed, power hungry and placed personal interests above the good of the whole. Thomas was given to doubt and dragged the morale of the group down. Matthew was at best an opportunist and at worst an extorter and traitor to his people. Simon, fondly referred to as the zealot, would have believed violence justifiable in the overthrow of Roman governance. Of course, there was Judas Iscariot, who betrayed Jesus for 30 pieces of silver. From a human perspective this is not a promising start for the church.

Yet, it was through these men that God established the church, and it is still through these types of men and women that he continues to work today. The good news is that the mission of the church does not depend solely upon any of us, but upon a supernatural resource, one who enables us to be effective witnesses wherever we go. Luke records Jesus' words in the opening to the book of Acts, as he explains the supernatural power available to be his witnesses.

Gathering them together, He commanded them not to leave Jerusalem, but to wait for what the Father had promised, "Which," He said, "you heard of from Me; for John baptized with water, but you will be baptized with the Holy Spirit not many days from now." So when they had come together, they were asking Him, saying, "Lord, is it at this time You are re storing the kingdom to Israel?" He said to them, "It is not for you to know times or epochs which the Father has fixed by His own authority; but you will receive power when the Holy Spirit has come upon you; and you shall be My witnesses both in Jerusalem, and in all Judea and Samaria, and even to the remotest part of the earth." Acts 1:4-8 (NASB)

Sending Out Disciples

John the Baptist was born to Zechariah and Elizabeth, six months before Jesus. Zechariah was a Jewish priest and Elizabeth was the cousin of Mary, Jesus' mother. In the Gospel of Matthew we learn that John's special ministry focused on calling Jews to repentance.

In those days John the Baptist came, preaching in the Desert of Judea and saying, "Repent, for the kingdom of heaven is near." Matthew 3:1-2 (NIV)

Prophets like John the Baptist placed emphasis on repentance, calling the nation of Israel back to God's law. As John called people to repentance he also baptized them in preparation for the ministry of the coming Messiah, a ministry that would provide the forgiveness of sins. In this way John's baptism was a symbol of the salvation yet to come through Jesus Christ, just as baptism is today a symbol of God's grace finally made available through faith in Christ. Yet Jesus drew a distinction between John's baptism of water and the baptism of the Holy Spirit. In fact, this distinction highlights the significance of the Holy Spirit's ministry and power in our lives.

John's call to repentance was a reminder to the Jewish people of their need to keep the law, specifically the Ten Commandments. The problem was that John's baptism did not bring any real and lasting change in the person's soul state, any more than water baptism does today. Being dunked does not change us at all, other than making us wet, which is not to say it does not serve a purpose. Baptism serves a vital purpose, proclaiming to the world our dependence upon Christ for the forgiveness of sin, but that is all it does. It only symbolizes the change, and Jesus is saying that he will offer a much more powerful baptism, one that actually produces real and lasting change in a person's life. In Hebrews we read of the change provided through Jesus.

> This is my covenant I will make with them after that time, says the Lord. I will put my laws in their hearts, and I will write them on their minds. Hebrews 10:16 (NIV)

Jesus wants us to know that our best opportunity for change is no longer John's baptism. John's ministry pointed out the need for repentance and forgiveness before God's law, while the baptism of the Holy Spirit actually enables us to keep the law. This means willpower and discipline are no longer our best resource for change. Our best opportunity for change comes as we receive the Holy Spirit. Willpower and discipline are valuable, but these activities are aimed at the fruit of the issues rather than the root. These activities, like John's baptism of water, only touch the surface of the problem, while the Holy Spirit works from the inside out, addressing the sinful desires of our heart.

This means that when we have something we want to see changed, we must learn not to simply throw more discipline and willpower at the problem. We should instead allow the Holy Spirit to change our desires, allowing the law that has been written on our heart and mind to work its way into our actions and attitudes. And when we are completely overwhelmed by sin and do not know what to ask for in prayer, we are comforted by the Holy Spirit, who prays on our behalf.

In the same way, the Spirit helps us in our weakness. We do not know what we ought to pray for, but the Spirit himself intercedes for us with groans that words cannot express. And he who searches our hearts knows the mind of the Spirit, because the Spirit intercedes for the saints in accordance with God's will. Romans 8:26-27 (NIV)

What does this have to do with the activity of *Sending Out Disciples*? The power necessary to live as witnesses is provided through the Holy Spirit. In fact, it was ultimately the transforming work brought by the Holy Spirit in the lives of the first disciples that offered some of the most convincing proof of the gospel's truth. Men who were previously full of doubt and thoughts of self-preservation were changed to men of faith and self-sacrifice. On the day of Pentecost Peter stood up and addressed a crowd of thousands to explain the grace of God offered through the death of Christ. Just a few weeks earlier it was Peter who had denied Christ three times.

Witnesses

There is a telling moment in the first few verses of the book of Acts, a moment in which we get a glimpse of the disciples' hearts and minds, just days before Pentecost. All along the disciples had wrongly assumed that the Messiah was going to be a political hero, rescuing Israel from its Roman oppressors. Upon hearing that the Holy Spirit was coming soon, they naturally assumed that Jesus was going to somehow use the Holy Spirit to reestablish the nation of Israel, but they were once again mistaken about God's purposes. Jesus said to them,

It is not for you to know the times and dates the Father has set by his own authority. But you will receive power when the Holy Spirit comes on you; and you will be my witnesses in Jerusalem, and in all Judea and Samaria, and to the ends of the earth. Acts 1:7-8 (NIV)

Instead of political ends, Jesus says that the power of the Holy Spirit is meant to enable us to be his witnesses. The primary purpose of the Spirit's transforming work in our lives is not simply for our benefit, so that we can see good things happen in our lives, so that our kingdoms grow larger and more prosperous. The primary purpose of the Spirit's transforming work in our lives is so that we can be Jesus' witnesses, so that we can reflect his character, conduct, and concerns in every area of our lives. God changes the hearts and minds of men and women, so that the world can see the power of the gospel lived out in the lives of Jesus' followers.

Once the Spirit comes upon the believers in Acts 2, their posture is uniquely and dramatically changed. They are no longer concerned about building a political kingdom, or even their own kingdoms, but they see the work of spreading the gospel as their primary mission, and they sacrifice everything for that purpose (Acts 4:32-37). Men and women whose hearts were previously full of doubt and whose minds were filled only with thoughts of self-interest, are changed to men and women of faith and self-sacrifice through the presence of the Holy Spirit in their lives.

Unfortunately many approach faith with selfish motives, believing that the transforming power of the Holy Spirit is some type of divine self-help system or method of self-improvement. This message is popularized through what is commonly known as the "health and wealth" gospel, which wrongly teaches that God is primarily concerned with our health and our material wealth. It is true the Spirit is at work in our lives to grow us and strengthen us, to make us holy, just as Christ is holy. But we are not an end in ourselves. The transforming work of the Holy Spirit in our lives is a means to a greater end—that is the spreading of the good news to the nations and bringing glory to God. No matter where you are in your faith journey, God offers you his Holy Spirit and invites you to be a part of building his kingdom.

Hitting the Target

Sending Out Disciples is an essential activity of a Disciplemaking church. Jesus described our heavenly Father as seeking the lost (Luke 14:22-24), and throughout history God has enlisted others to share in that work. In the Old Testament God sent Moses to deliver the Israelites from bondage, and he sent prophets to call the Israelites back to repentance. In the New Testament God sent his Son to die on a cross, and Jesus sent out the first 12 disciples, as well as another 72 later in his ministry (Matthew 10:7-8, Luke 10:1,3). At the end of his ministry, Jesus commissioned all of his followers to go and make disciples (Matthew 28:19-20), and the early church set apart missionaries for the purpose of carrying the gospel to foreign lands (Acts 13:2-3). Disciples are a people sent out, which means that Disciplemaking churches are to be sending people out. Jesus even instructed his followers to pray that God would provide more workers for the harvest fields (Matthew 9:37-38), more people to go.

When the church sends out disciples it sends them out to do two activities primarily, *Pursue the Lost Intentionally* and *Love Others Selflessly,* which are the seventh and eighth attributes of a disciple and are described in chapters 9 and 10. The attribute of pursuing the lost is conversion ministry (i.e. evangelism), while the attribute of loving others selflessly is compassion ministry. Just as God pursued us through Christ and while we were still sinners, we are to pursue others, with the message of the gospel and with a demonstration of Christ's selfless and sacrificial love.

Jesus said, "By this all men will know that you are my disciples, if you love one another" (John 13:35). Jesus said, "My command is this: Love each other as I have loved you" (John 15:12). According to Scripture, we are to give our lives away to others through acts of compassion and mercy, just as Jesus has given his life for us. God's love for us, demonstrated on the cross and experienced in salvation, will draw us out of selfish and self-seeking lifestyles and motivate us to lay our lives down for others.

The good news of the gospel is that God is asking us to do only what he has already done for us, and the more we are in touch with his sacrifice on our behalf the more we are motivated to follow in his footsteps.

What makes a church a part of The Church? What distinguishing markers help us identify the people of God? What is to set Christians apart from non-Christians and the church of Christ apart from other non-profit social institutions? How are we different than the park district or the school district or the federal government? In Acts we read that within the early church no one "claimed anything as his own, but rather everything was held in common." The result of this type of compassion was that the message of the gospel was preached "with great power" (Acts 4:32-35).

Conclusion

We are not an end in ourselves. The transforming work of the Holy Spirit is a means to a greater end—that is our being God's witnesses to the nations. We were saved to bring God glory through the spread of the gospel. The gospel is spread through both a verbal proclamation of the good news and a physical demonstration of Jesus' selfless and sacrificial love.

133

Group Discussion Questions

1. Considering the character deficits of the first disciples, in what respects are you similarly ill-equipped to contribute to God's work?

2. When/how have you resorted to relying simply on willpower or discipline to bring about change in your life rather than upon God's Spirit?

3. How are we to rely upon God's Spirit for transformation, and how is this compatible with acting responsibly? (John 15:4)

4. In what ways have you experienced God's transforming work in your life? (2 Corinthians 5:17)

5. How has God's transformation of your character strengthened your witness?

6. To where and/or to whom has God sent you to be his witness?

7. What sending effort within your church can you be a part of in the days ahead?

8. How would you like people to be praying for you as you work to apply what you have learned in this chapter to your life?

9. How can you be praying for your church's effort to send out disciples?

Sources

Chapter 1
1. Chesterton, G.K. *What's Wrong with the World*, chapter 5.

Chapter 2
1. Lewis, C.S. *The Weight of Glory.*
2. Pippert, Rebecca. *Out of the Salt Shaker*, 12.
3. Claiborne, Shane. *The Irresistible Revolution*, 43.
4. Lewis, C.S. *Letters to Malcolm*
5. Chesterton, G.K. *Orthodoxy*, 58.

Chapter 3
1. Yancey, Philip. *What's So Amazing About Grace*, 15.
2. "United States v. Wilson, 32 U.S. 150 (1833)" accessed January 2011, http://supreme.justia.com/us/32/150/case.html.

Chapter 6
1. Bonhoeffer, Dietrich. *Life Together: The Classic Exploration of Faith in Community*, 27.

Chapter 7
1. "Mark Twain Quotations, Newspaper Collections, & Related Resources" accessed January 2011, http://www.twainquotes.com.

Chapter 8
1. Kierkegaard, Soren. *Provocations: Spiritual Writings of Kierkegaard*. Charles E. Moore, ed., 201.

Chapter 9
1. Chesterton, G.K. *What's Wrong with the World,* chapter 5.

Chapter 10
1. Thompson, Francis. *The Hound of Heaven.*
2. Adapted from *Following Christ* by Joseph M. Stowell, 130-131.

MY DIRTY SHIRT
A Modern Parable of Salvation

My Dirty Shirt is a parable of one man's search for freedom from sin, as well as the story of every man's opportunity to escape from the guilt, shame and suffering brought by sin.

Most of the world's religions are summed up by the single word "do." Whether it is the education of humanists or the Karma of eastern religions or the prayer and fasting required in Islam, all religions tell us to just scrub harder in order to remove the stain of sin. Religions provide the framework for cleaning like laundromats provide machines and detergents, but ultimately we are the ones that do the work.

The Gospel of Jesus Christ, however, is summed up by the singular word "done." Christianity is categorically different than all other religions, as Christians are not trusting in their ability to remove the stain of sin from their life but in the finished work of Jesus Christ on the cross.

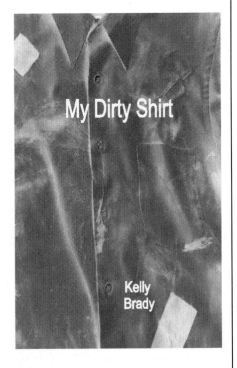

This modern parable explains the difference between Christianity and the other major world religions. My hope is that many will accept the invitation to wear another man's shirt, just as I have. For more information visit www.equippedtoserve.org.

POCKET THEOLOGY
A guide to the Bible's teaching for those on the go...

People have lots of questions about what the Bible teaches, but very little time. *Pocket Theology* provides answers for those on the go. Whether you are a non-Christian, wanting to learn more about what the Bible teaches, a Christian parent wanting to be better prepared to answer the questions your children are asking, or a leader within the church needing a quick reference guide, this book is for you.

As a pastor, I am daily reminded that shepherds do not grow the grass. They just point to it. When caring for others our job is to point to God's Word, because the greatest need we all have is to hear the truth of God's Word.

This book is designed as a quick reference tool, offering both a concise theological summary on a broad range of topics, as well as Scripture references for those who want to do further study. Sprinkled throughout the book are answers to some of the most common questions that people ask about the Christian faith. Questions like: Why are there so many different versions of the Bible? And Why are there so many different Christian denominations? Visit www.equippedtoserve.org for more information.

GLEN ELLYN BIBLE CHURCH
ELDER NOTEBOOK
A Manuel Strengthening Elder Leadership

What do you think of when you hear the word "Elder"? Do you think of long hours in church committee meetings, fundraisers and financial officers, or advisors to the pastoral staff?

According to the New Testament, Elders are those charged by God with the care of his people (1 Peter 5:1-2). Peter wrote that Elders are the shepherds of God's flock, which includes guarding the church's doctrine, disciplining those within the flock who need correction or encouragement to live lives of godliness, as well as setting the church's direction by cultivating and casting the church's ministry vision.

Peter highlights the breadth and depth of Elder responsibilities in a single verse writing, "Therefore, I exhort the <u>Elders</u> (presbutoros) among you...to <u>shepherd</u> (poimen) the flock of God among you, exercising <u>oversight</u> (episkopos)" (1 Peter 5:1-2, NASB). These three terms together give us a picture of the role Elders are to play in the local congregation. They are to wisely and maturely govern the church (presbutoros), exer-

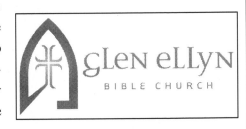

cise authority and manage ministry (episkopos), as well as care for and direct people spiritually (poimen).

With such a high call it is important to firmly grasp the qualifications and the responsibilities of Elder leadership and this detailed manual gives specific directions on how Elders are to carry out these responsibilities. Visit www.equippedtoserve.org for more information.